Spanish

GRADE 3

Published by Brighter Child®
an imprint of Carson-Dellosa Publishing LLC
Greensboro, NC

Pronunciation Key

Use the pronunciation key below to learn how to say and make the sound of each Spanish letter.

Spanish Letter	English Pronunciation of Letter	The Sound the Letter Makes	Example of the Letter Sound
a	ah	ah	p<u>o</u>t
b	be	b	<u>b</u>at
c	say	k or s	<u>c</u>at, <u>c</u>ity
d	de	d	<u>d</u>og
e	eh	e	p<u>e</u>t
f	efe	f, ph	<u>f</u>oot
g	hey	g, h	<u>g</u>o, <u>h</u>and
h	ache	silent	silent
i	ee	ee	f<u>ee</u>t
j	hota	h	<u>h</u>ot
k	ka	k	ca<u>k</u>e
l	ele	l	<u>l</u>emon
m	eme	m	<u>m</u>ind
n	ene	n	<u>n</u>o
ñ	eñe	ñ	o<u>n</u>ion
o	o	o	b<u>o</u>at
p	pe	p	<u>p</u>ot
q	ku	ku	<u>c</u>ool
r	ere	r	<u>r</u>obe
s	ese	s	<u>s</u>o
t	te	t	<u>t</u>oe
u	oo	oo	p<u>oo</u>l
v	ve	v	<u>v</u>ine
w	doblay-oo	w	<u>w</u>e
x	equis	ks	e<u>x</u>it
y	ee griega	y	<u>y</u>ellow
z	seta	s	<u>s</u>uit

Note: The letters "t" and "d" are pronounced with the tongue slightly between the teeth and not behind the teeth.

Brighter Child®
An imprint of Carson-Dellosa Publishing LLC
P.O. Box 35665
Greensboro, NC 27425 USA

Printed in the USA • All rights reserved.   ISBN 0-7696-7633-2

05-203137784

Table of Contents

Numbers Crossword 4
Numbers 5
Numbers Illustration 6
Who Is It? 7
Masculine and Feminine 8
It's a Small World 9
Pretty Colors 10
Words to Describe 11
Words to Describe 12
Action Words 13
Action Figures 14
Greetings Paste Up 15
What's Your Name? 16
Word Blocks 17
Greetings 18
Spanish Greetings 19
Yesterday and Today 20
Rain in April 21
Writing Practice 22
Birds of Color 23
House of Colors 24
Color the Flowers 25
Moving Colors 26
Color Crossword 27
Colorful Flowers 28
Draw and Color 29
Butterfly Garden 30
Across the Spectrum 31
Food Words 32
Food Riddles 33
Use the Clues 34
A Square Meal 35
Eat It Up 36
Use the Clues 37

Three Little Kittens 38
Animal Match 39
Clothes to Color 40
Clothes Closet 41
Dressing Up 42
Matching Clothes 43
Face Riddles 44
A Blank Face 45
How Are You? 46
Happy Faces 47
Matching Family 48
Family Ties 49
My Family 50
Family Tree 51
Places, Please 52
A Place for Riddles 53
Where Am I? 54
Fitting In 55
Around the House 56
Around the Block 57
Around the House 58
Match Words and Pictures 59
Use the Clues 60
Around the Room 61
A Fitting Design 62
Classroom Clutter 63
Show and Tell 64
Songs and Chants 65
Songs 66
Learning Cards 67
Learning Cards 68
Learning Cards 69
Learning Cards 70
Answer Key 71–80

Numbers Crossword

Use the words at the bottom to help you with this crossword puzzle. Write the Spanish number words in the puzzle spaces. Follow the English clues.

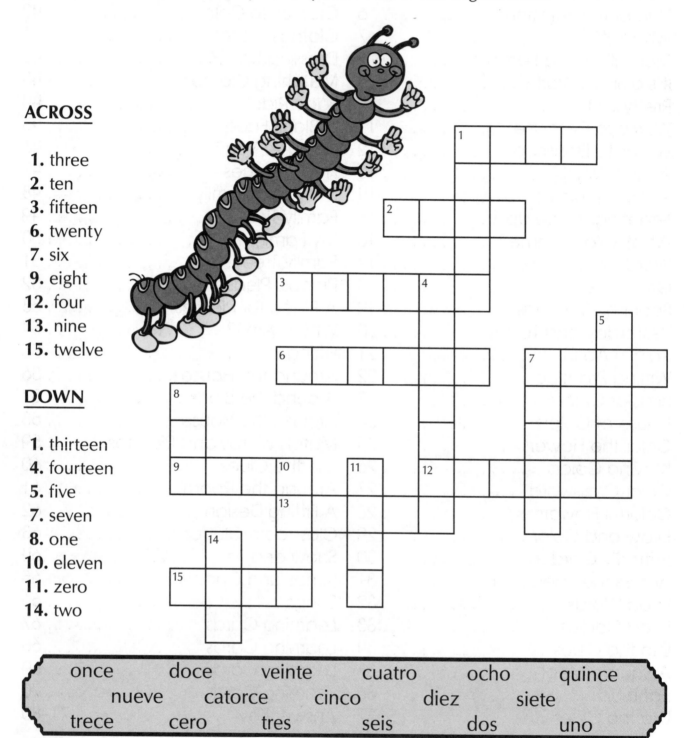

ACROSS

1. three
2. ten
3. fifteen
6. twenty
7. six
9. eight
12. four
13. nine
15. twelve

DOWN

1. thirteen
4. fourteen
5. five
7. seven
8. one
10. eleven
11. zero
14. two

once   doce   veinte   cuatro   ocho   quince
nueve   catorce   cinco   diez   siete
trece   cero   tres   seis   dos   uno

Numbers

After each numeral, write the number word in Spanish. Refer to the words below to help you.

Word Bank

veinte	cuatro	nueve	diez	diecisiete	quince
doce	once	trece	siete	uno	tres
catorce	dos	cero	ocho	cinco	dieciséis
diecinueve		dieciocho		seis	

0 _____

1 _____

2 _____

3 _____

4 _____

5 _____

6 _____

7 _____

8 _____

9 _____

10 _____

11 _____

12 _____

13 _____

14 _____

15 _____

16 _____

17 _____

18 _____

19 _____

20 _____

Spanish: Grade 3

Numbers Illustration

Write the number. Draw that many things in the box. The first one is done for you.

☆☆☆☆ ☆☆☆☆ **ocho** means __8__	**cinco** means _____	**diecisiete** means _____
doce means _____	**uno** means _____	**dos** means _____
catorce means _____	**nueve** means _____	**veinte** means _____
siete means _____	**cuatro** means _____	**quince** means _____

Who Is It?

Write the names of people you may know that fit each description below.

tú–informal or familiar form of you	
someone you refer to by first name	
your sister or brother (or cousin)	
a classmate	
a close friend	
a child younger than yourself	

usted–formal or polite form of you	
someone with a title	
an older person	
a stranger	
a person of authority	

How would you speak to each person below? Write *tú* or *usted* after each person named.

1. Dr. Hackett _____

2. Susana _____

3. a four-year-old _____

4. your grandfather _____

5. the governor _____

6. your best friend _____

7. your sister _____

8. the principal _____

9. a classmate _____

10. a stranger _____

Masculine and Feminine

All Spanish nouns and adjectives have gender. This means they are either masculine or feminine. Here are two basic rules to help determine the gender of words. There are other rules for gender which you will learn as you study more Spanish.

1. Spanish words ending in -o are usually masculine.
2. Spanish words ending in -a are usually feminine.

Write the following words in the charts to determine their gender. Write the English meanings to the right. Use a Spanish-English dictionary if you need help.

maestra	libro	escritorio	negro	abrigo	sopa	tienda
amigo	ventana	pluma	maestro	vestido	fruta	museo
silla	puerta	anaranjado	amiga	camisa	queso	casa
rojo	cuaderno	blanco	falda	chaqueta		

Masculine		Feminine	
words ending in -o	meaning of the word	words ending in -a	meaning of the word

It's a Small World

In Spanish, there are four ways to say "the"—*el, la, los,* and *las.* The definite article (the) agrees with its noun in gender (masculine or feminine) and number (singular or plural).

Masculine singular nouns go with *el.* Feminine singular nouns go with *la.*

Examples: *el libro* (the book)   *el papel* (the paper)
                  la silla (the chair)   *la regla* (the ruler)

Masculine plural nouns go with *los.* Feminine plural nouns go with *las.*

Examples: *los libros* (the books)   *los papeles* (the papers)
                  las sillas (the chairs)   *las reglas* (the rulers)

Refer to the Word Bank to complete the chart. Write the singular and plural forms and the correct definite articles. The first ones have been done for you.

Word Bank				
cuaderno	mesa	pluma	oso	falda
papel	gato	bota	silla	libro

English	Masculine Singular	Masculine Plural
the book	el libro	los libros
the paper		
the notebook		
the cat		
the bear		

English	Feminine Singular	Feminine Plural
the chair	la silla	las sillas
the table		
the boot		
the skirt		
the pen		

Pretty Colors

Adjectives are words that tell about or describe nouns. Color each box as indicated in Spanish. Use a Spanish-English dictionary if you need help.

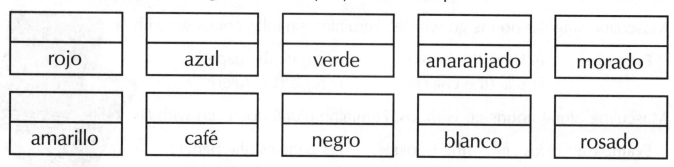

| rojo | azul | verde | anaranjado | morado |

| amarillo | café | negro | blanco | rosado |

Here are some new adjectives. Copy the Spanish adjectives in the boxes. Write the Spanish words next to the English at the bottom of the page.

bonita	pretty	feo	ugly
grande	big	pequeño	small
limpio	clean	sucio	dirty
viejo	old	nuevo	new
alegre	happy	triste	sad

old _____   pretty _____   sad _____

big _____   small _____   happy _____

new _____   dirty _____   ugly _____

clean _____

Words to Describe

Descriptive adjectives are words that describe nouns. Refer to the Word Bank to write the Spanish adjective that describes each picture.

Word Bank

alegre	grande	nuevo	pequeño	feo	rico
limpio	sucio	bonita	triste	viejo	pobre
alto	bajo	abierto	cerrado		

large

new

ugly

happy

old

sad

small

clean

pretty

dirty

tall

open

rich

short

closed

poor

Spanish: Grade 3

Words to Describe

Write the Spanish words for the clue words in the crossword puzzle.

Across

3. poor
7. open
9. tall
11. clean
12. dirty
13. new

Down

1. ugly
2. closed
4. happy
5. pretty
6. large
8. old
10. sad

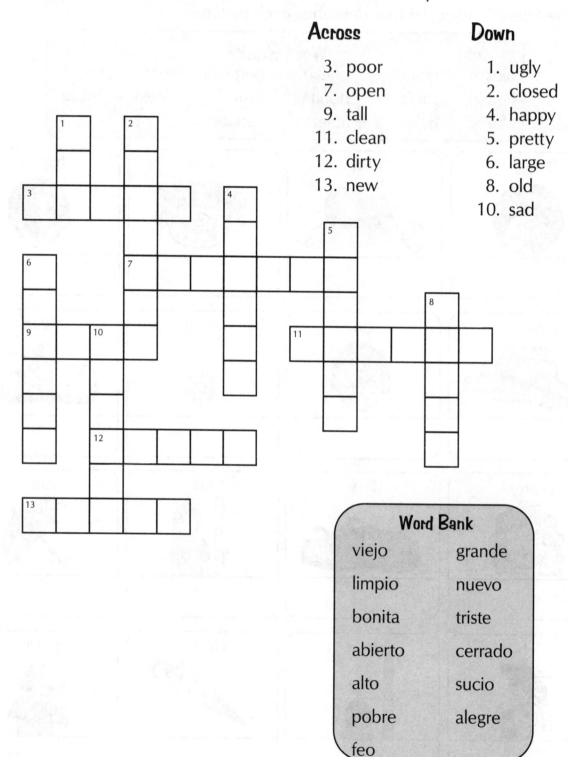

Word Bank

viejo	grande
limpio	nuevo
bonita	triste
abierto	cerrado
alto	sucio
pobre	alegre
feo	

Action Words

In each box, copy the Spanish action verb. Then, write the English word below it.

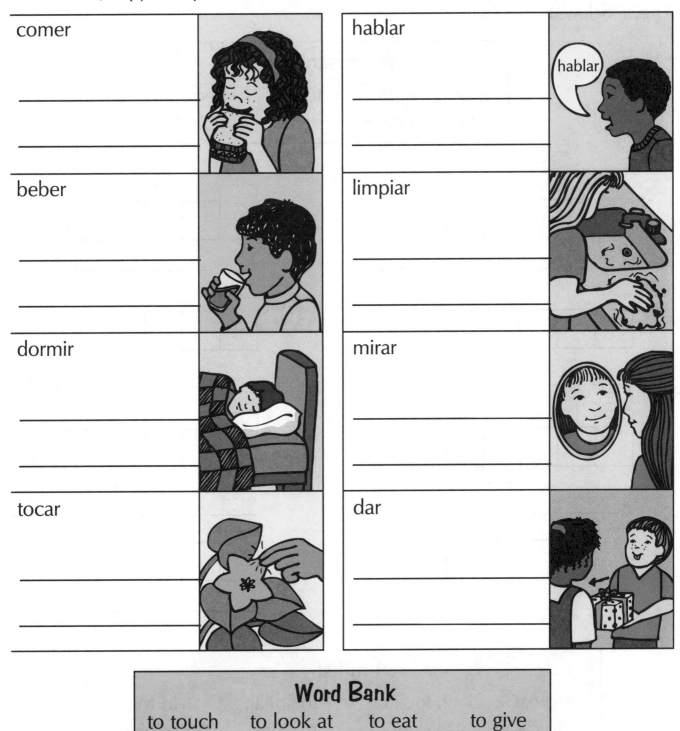

comer
_____
_____

hablar
_____
_____

beber
_____
_____

limpiar
_____
_____

dormir
_____
_____

mirar
_____
_____

tocar
_____
_____

dar
_____
_____

Word Bank

to touch	to look at	to eat	to give
to drink	to speak	to clean	to sleep

Action Figures

Write the Spanish words from the Word Bank that fit in these word blocks. Write the English below the blocks.

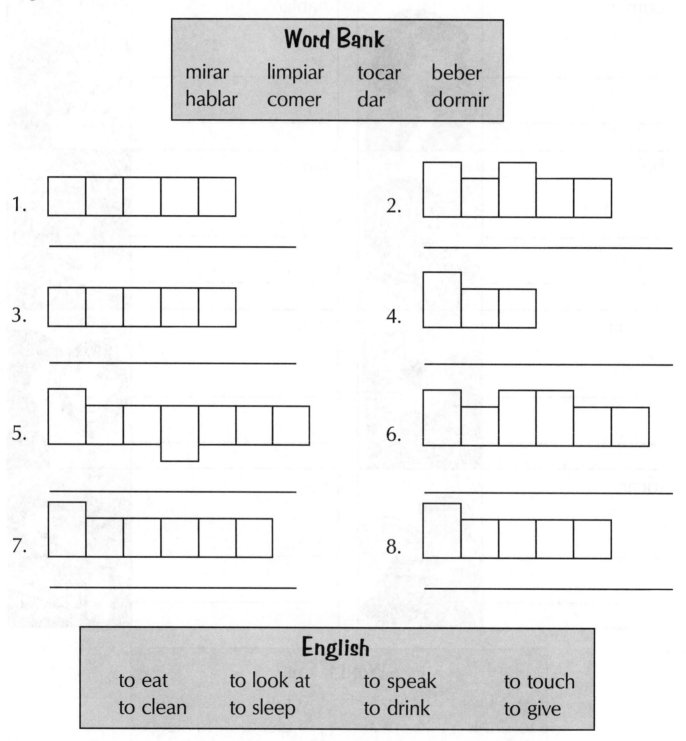

Word Bank

mirar	limpiar	tocar	beber
hablar	comer	dar	dormir

1. _____

2. _____

3. _____

4. _____

5. _____

6. _____

7. _____

8. _____

English

to eat	to look at	to speak	to touch
to clean	to sleep	to drink	to give

Greetings Paste Up

Cut out a picture from a magazine that shows the meaning of each greeting and glue it next to the correct word or words.

¡Hola!

¿Cómo te llamas?

Me llamo...

¿Cómo estás?

bien

mal

así, así

¡Adiós!

What's Your Name?

Word Bank

I'm so-so.	What's your name?	I'm well/fine.
I'm ____ years old.	I'm not doing well.	My name is ___.
I'm not well.	How are you?	How old are you?

Refer to the Word Bank to translate the Spanish questions and answers into English.

1. ¿Cómo te llamas? _____

   Me llamo _____. _____

2. ¿Cómo estás? _____

   Estoy bien/mal/así así. _____

3. ¿Cuántos años tienes? _____

   Tengo ___ años. _____

Word Bank

hello	please	friend	yes
no	thank you	goodbye	See you later!

Write the English meaning after the Spanish word.

4. hola _____

5. amigo, amiga _____

6. sí _____

7. no _____

8. por favor _____

9. gracias _____

10. ¡Hasta luego! _____

11. adiós _____

Word Blocks

Write the Spanish words from the Word Bank that fit in these word blocks. Don't forget the punctuation. Write the English meanings below the blocks.

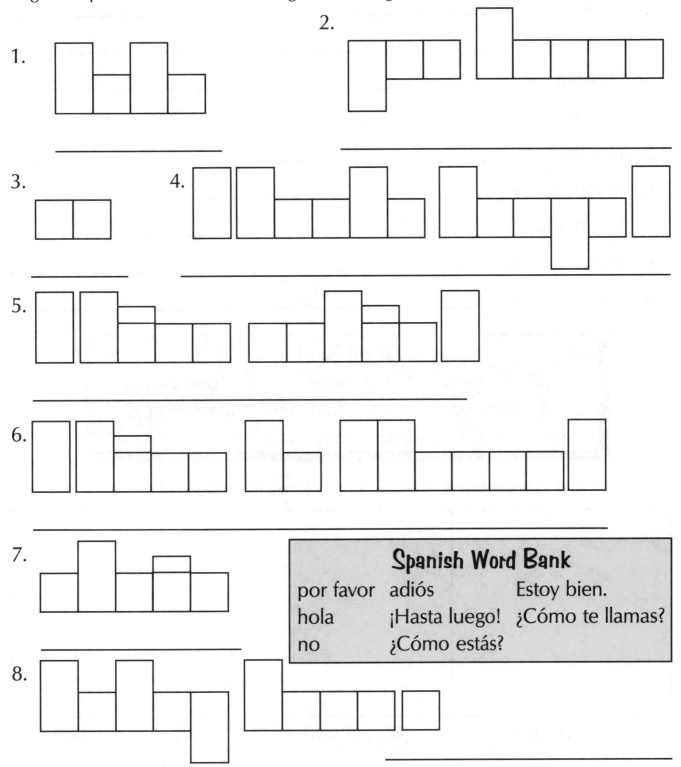

Spanish Word Bank

por favor	adiós	Estoy bien.
hola	¡Hasta luego!	¿Cómo te llamas?
no	¿Cómo estás?	

Greetings

Write the English meaning of the Spanish words and phrases.

1. señor _____

2. señora _____

3. señorita _____

4. maestro _____

5. maestra _____

6. ¡Buenos días! _____

7. ¡Buenas tardes! _____

8. ¡Buenas noches! _____

9. Vamos a contar. _____

Word Bank

Mr.	Good night!	Good morning!
Good afternoon!	teacher (female)	teacher (male)
Miss	Let's count.	Mrs.

Draw a picture to show the time of day that you use each expression.

¡Buenos días!	¡Buenas tardes!	¡Buenas noches!

Name _____

Spanish Greetings

Write the Spanish word for each clue in the crossword puzzle.

Across

1. bad
4. good
7. teacher (male)
9. friend (female)
10. Mr.
11. Miss

Down

2. friend (male)
3. hello
5. thank you
6. goodbye
7. teacher (female)
8. Mrs.

Word Bank

amiga	mal
señora	señor
maestra	bien
adiós	hola
señorita	gracias
amigo	maestro

Name _____

Yesterday and Today

Write the Spanish words for the days of the week. Remember, in Spanish-speaking countries, Monday is the first day of the week.

Word Bank		
miércoles	jueves	sábado
viernes	lunes	martes
	domingo	

Monday _____

Tuesday _____

Wednesday _____

Thursday _____

Friday _____

Saturday _____

Sunday _____

If today is Monday, yesterday was Sunday. Complete the following chart by identifying the missing days in Spanish. The first one is done for you.

ayer (yesterday)	hoy (today)	mañana (tomorrow)
martes	miércoles	jueves
lunes		
		sábado
	domingo	
	jueves	
		martes
viernes		

Rain in April

Refer to the Word Bank to write the Spanish word for the given month. Then, in the box, draw a picture of something that happens in that month of the year. Remember that Spanish months do not begin with capital letters.

Word Bank

agosto	septiembre	noviembre	mayo
junio	enero	octubre	febrero
marzo	julio	diciembre	abril

January _____		July _____	
February _____		August _____	
March _____		September _____	
April _____		October _____	
May _____		November _____	
June _____		December _____	

Writing Practice

Copy the following paragraph in your best handwriting. Practice reading it out loud.

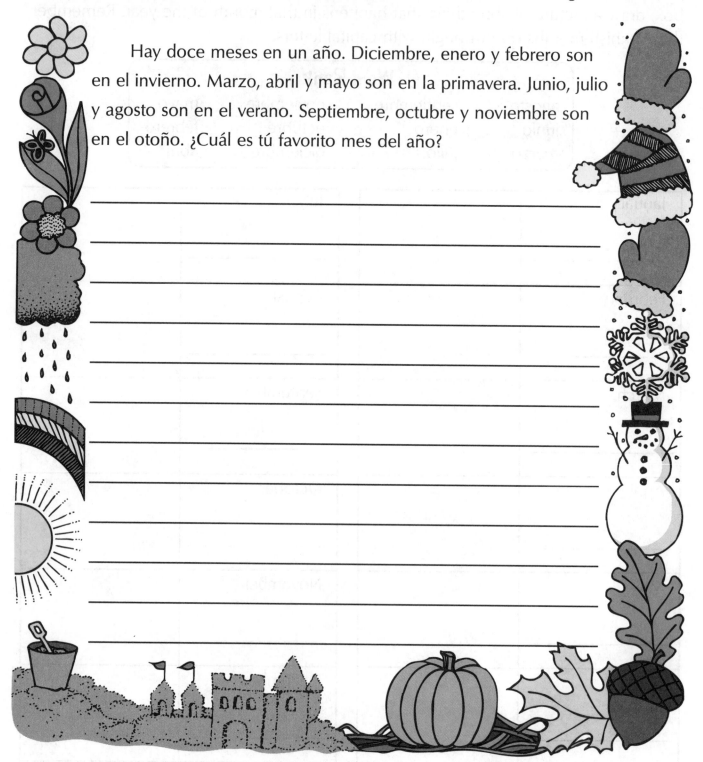

Hay doce meses en un año. Diciembre, enero y febrero son
en el invierno. Marzo, abril y mayo son en la primavera. Junio, julio
y agosto son en el verano. Septiembre, octubre y noviembre son
en el otoño. ¿Cuál es tú favorito mes del año?

Birds of Color

Color the birds according to the words listed.

azul

café

morado

rosado

rojo

verde

negro

amarillo

anaranjado

House of Colors

Color each crayon with the correct color for the Spanish word. Add something with your favorite color.

☐ rojo ☐ negro ☐ café ☐ rosado
☐ azul ☐ amarillo ☐ blanco ☐ verde

Color the Flowers

Color each flower with the correct color for the Spanish word.

☐ azul ☐ café ☐ amarillo ☐ rosado
☐ verde ☐ rojo ☐ morado ☐ anaranjado

Spanish: Grade 3

Moving Colors

Color the pictures according to the words listed.

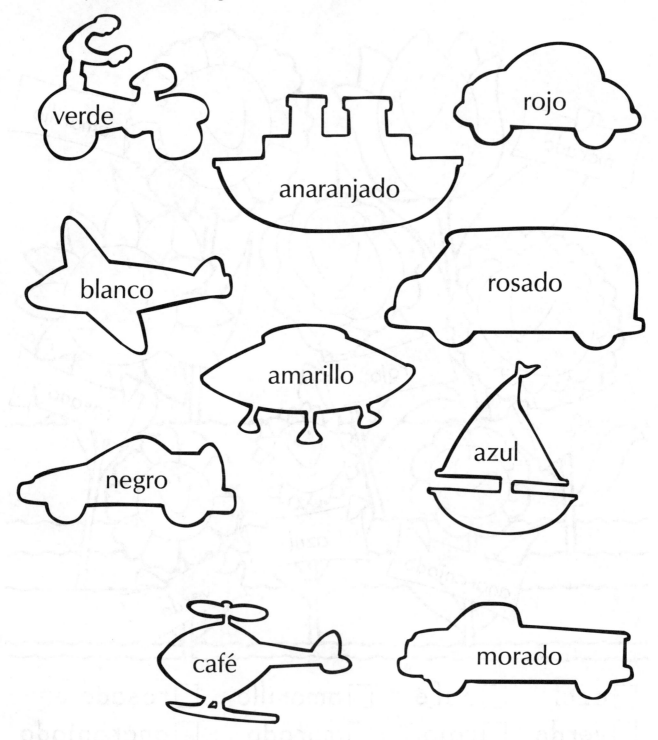

What is your favorite color? (Answer in Spanish.) _____

Color Crossword

Write the correct Spanish color words in the spaces.
Follow the English color clues.

ACROSS

3. yellow

5. purple

6. black

8. white

10. pink

DOWN

1. blue

2. red

4. orange

7. green

9. brown

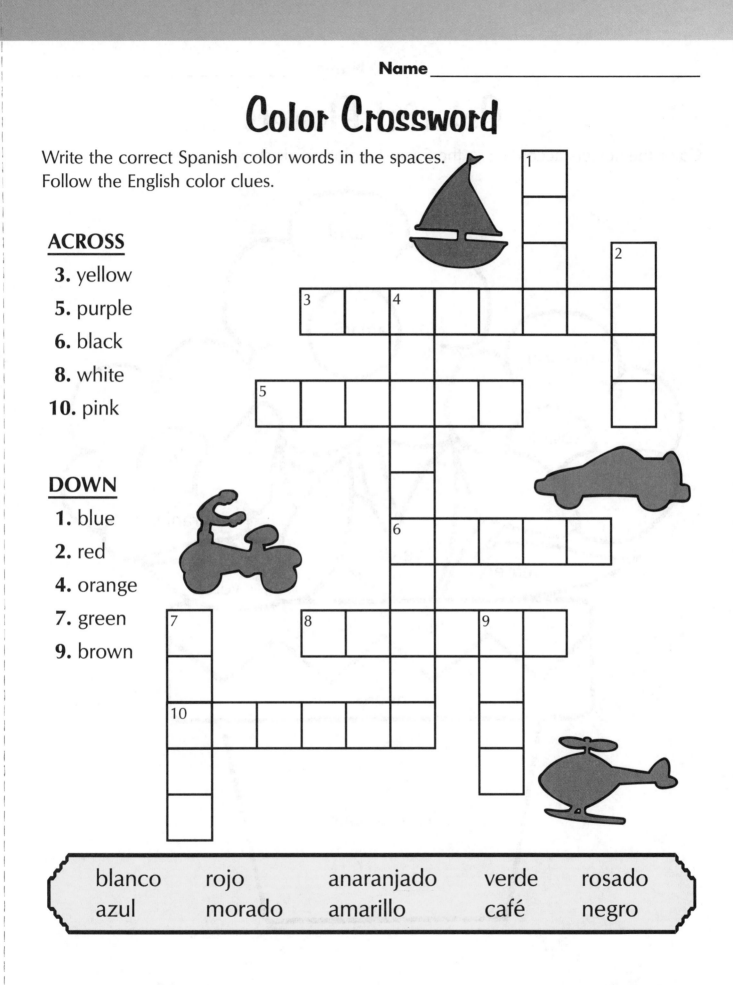

blanco   rojo   anaranjado   verde   rosado

azul   morado   amarillo   café   negro

Spanish: Grade 3

Colorful Flowers

Color the flowers according to the Spanish color words shown.

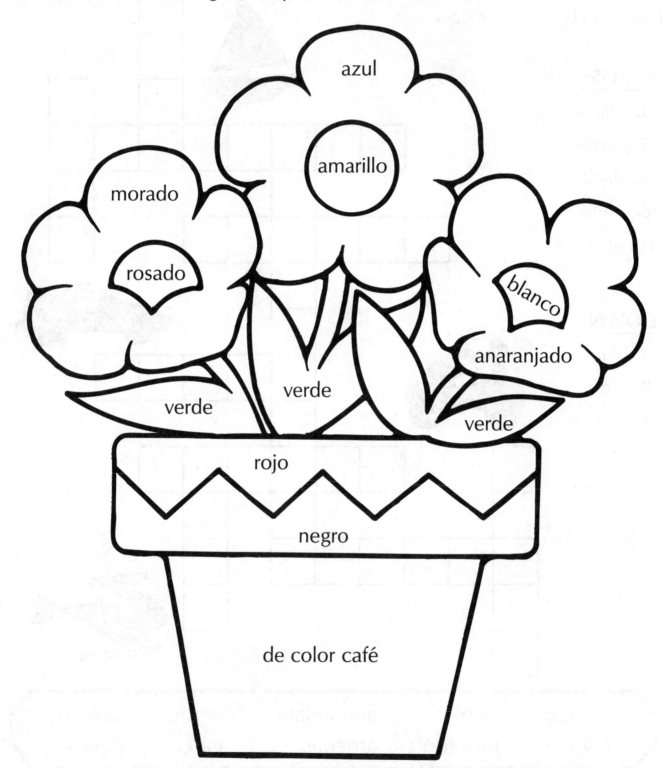

28

Draw and Color

In each box, write the Spanish color word. Use the Word Bank below to help you. Then, draw and color a picture of something that is usually that color.

red is _____	orange is _____	brown is _____
blue is _____	purple is _____	black is _____
green is _____	yellow is _____	pink is _____

Which Spanish color from the Word Bank is not used above? _____

Word Bank

blanco	rojo	amarillo	rosado
azul	morado	verde	negro
	anaranjado	café	

Butterfly Garden

Color the butterfly garden as indicated in Spanish.

anaranjado

morado

rojo

negro

azul

amarillo

verde

blanco

verde

rosado

verde

café

Name _____

Across the Spectrum

Write the Spanish for each clue word in the crossword puzzle.

Across

2. blue
4. brown
6. red
7. purple
8. white
9. black

Down

1. green
2. yellow
3. pink
5. orange

Spanish: Grade 3

Food Words

Say each word out loud. Write the English word next to it.

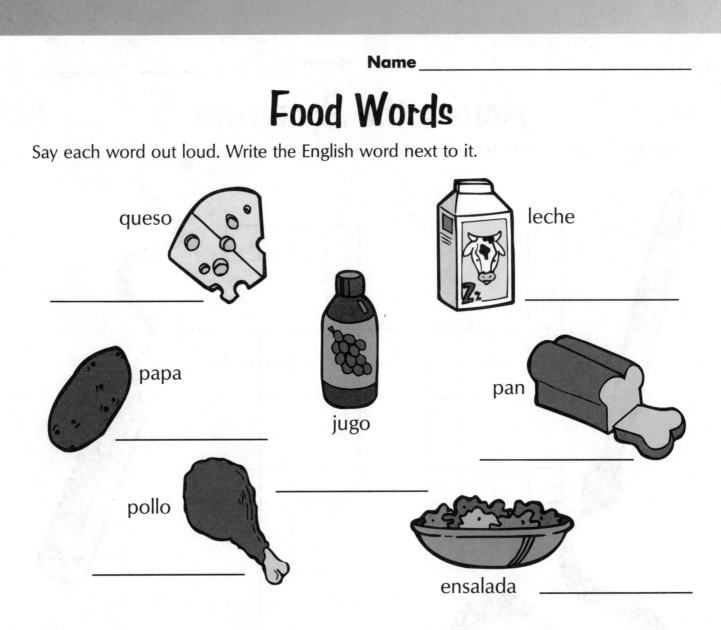

queso

_____

leche

_____

papa

_____

jugo

pan

_____

pollo

_____

ensalada _____

Color the blocks with letters.
Do not color the blocks with numbers. What word did you find? _____

7	x	7	7	7	7	7	7	7	7	7	x	7	7	7	7	7	7	7
7	x	7	7	7	7	7	7	7	7	7	x	7	7	7	7	7	7	7
7	x	7	7	7	7	7	7	7	7	7	x	7	7	7	7	7	7	7
7	x	7	x	x	x	7	x	x	x	7	x	7	7	7	x	x	x	7
7	x	7	x	7	x	7	x	7	7	7	x	x	x	7	x	7	x	7
7	x	7	x	x	x	7	x	7	7	7	x	7	x	7	x	x	x	7
7	x	7	x	7	7	7	x	7	7	7	x	7	x	7	x	7	7	7
7	x	7	x	x	x	7	x	x	x	7	x	7	x	7	x	x	x	7

Food Riddles

Answer the riddles. Use the size and shape of the word blocks along with the answers at the bottom to help you.

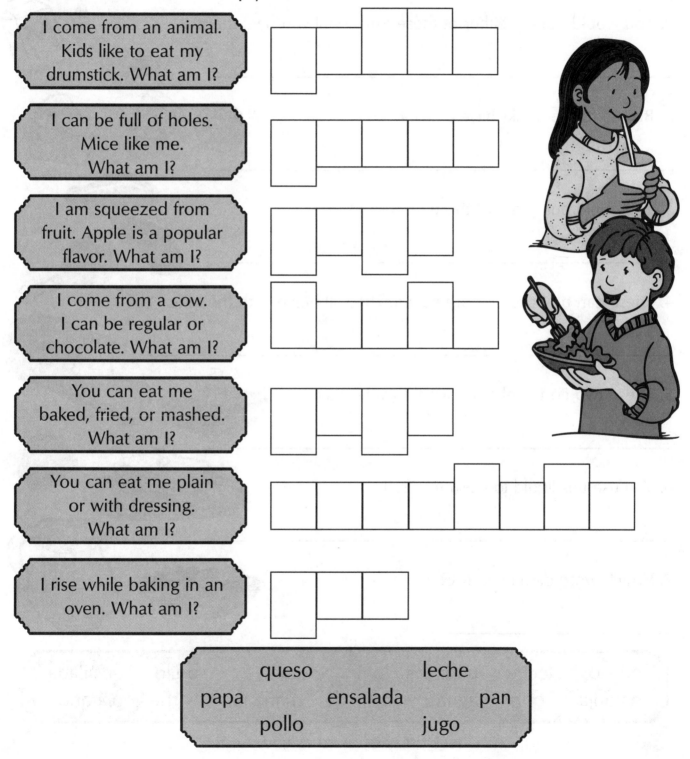

I come from an animal. Kids like to eat my drumstick. What am I?

I can be full of holes. Mice like me. What am I?

I am squeezed from fruit. Apple is a popular flavor. What am I?

I come from a cow. I can be regular or chocolate. What am I?

You can eat me baked, fried, or mashed. What am I?

You can eat me plain or with dressing. What am I?

I rise while baking in an oven. What am I?

queso   leche
papa   ensalada   pan
pollo   jugo

Use the Clues

Use the clues and the Word Bank at the bottom of the page to find the answers.
Do not use any answer more than once.

1. You would not eat either of these fruits until you peel them.

_____   _____

2. Both of these drinks have a flavor.

_____   _____

3. You could put either of these on a sandwich.

_____   _____

4. These can be baked before eating. They all begin with the letter "p."

_____   _____   _____

5. These two go together on a cold winter day.

_____   _____

6. You use this liquid to wash this fruit.

_____   _____

7. Which word didn't you use?

_____

queso	leche	papa	jugo	pan	pollo	ensalada
naranja	sopa	agua	sandwich	manzana	carne	plátano

Check off each word as you use it.

A Square Meal

Refer to the Word Bank to write the name of each food in Spanish.

Word Bank

queso	vegetales
leche	naranja
papa	sopa
pan	agua
jugo	sandwich
pollo	manzana
ensalada	carne
fruta	plátano

Spanish: Grade 3

Eat It Up

Write the Spanish for the clue words in the crossword puzzle.

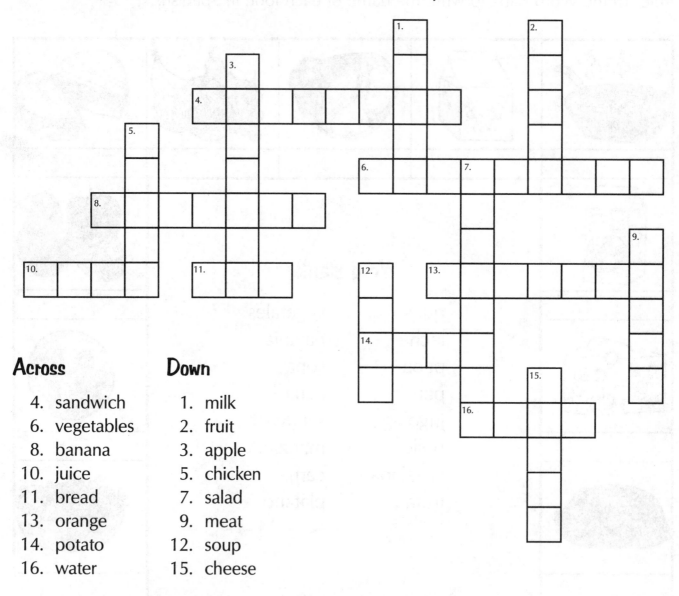

Across

4. sandwich
6. vegetables
8. banana
10. juice
11. bread
13. orange
14. potato
16. water

Down

1. milk
2. fruit
3. apple
5. chicken
7. salad
9. meat
12. soup
15. cheese

Word Bank

ensalada	plátano	manzana	papa
pan	naranja	fruta	queso
carne	sopa	jugo	vegetales
sandwich	leche	agua	pollo

Use the Clues

Answer the questions. Use the clues and the Spanish words at the bottom of the page. You may use answers more than once.

1. Both words begin with the same letter, and both animals have feathers.

_____   _____

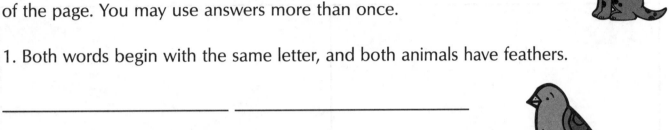

2. These two animals walk and are house pets.

_____   _____

3. Both animals begin with the same letter. One quacks and the other barks.

_____   _____

4. Both of these animals like to live in the water.

_____   _____

5. These animals do not have fur or feathers.

_____   _____

6. The first animal likes to chase and catch the second animal. They both end with the letter o.

_____   _____

gato	perro	pájaro
pez	pato	culebra

Three Little Kittens

Draw a picture to match the Spanish phrase in each box.

seis pájaros	cuatro perros
nueve abejas	siete osos
tres gatos	dos vacas
cinco patos	ocho caballos
diez ranas	un pez

Animal Match

Copy the Spanish word under each picture.

oso

rana

caballo

vaca

_____

elefante

oveja

puerco

gallina

_____

gato

tortuga

mariposa

dinosaurio

_____

Write the Spanish for each animal name.

1. butterfly _____

2. sheep _____

3. cat _____

4. dinosaur _____

5. chicken _____

6. pig _____

7. cow _____

8. bear _____

9. elephant _____

10. horse _____

11. turtle _____

12. frog _____

Spanish: Grade 3

Clothes to Color

Cut out pictures and glue them next to the correct words.

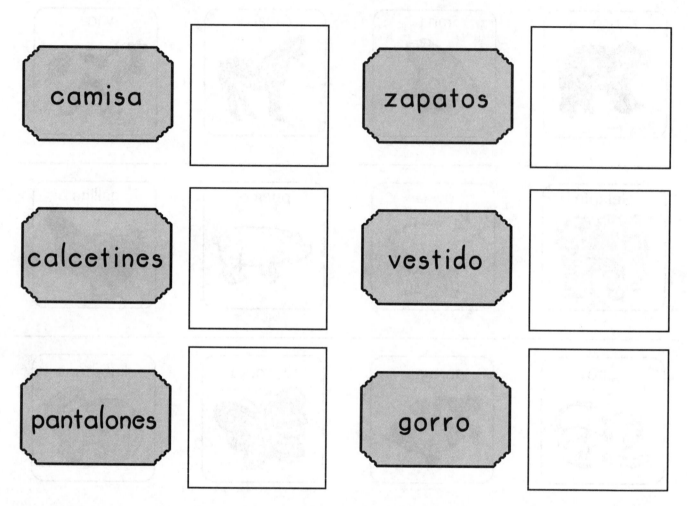

camisa

zapatos

calcetines

vestido

pantalones

gorro

Try this: Color each block with a letter X inside. Do not color the blocks with numbers. What hidden word did you find? _____

8	8	8	8	8	8	8	8	8	8	8	8	8	8	8	8	8	8	8	8	8	8
8	8	x	x	x	8	x	x	x	8	x	x	x	8	x	x	x	8	x	x	x	8
8	8	x	8	x	8	x	8	x	8	x	8	x	8	x	8	x	8	x	8	x	8
8	8	x	x	x	8	x	8	x	8	x	8	8	8	x	8	8	8	x	8	x	8
8	8	8	8	x	8	x	x	x	8	x	8	8	8	x	8	8	8	x	x	x	8
8	8	x	8	x	8	8	8	8	8	8	8	8	8	x	8	8	8	8	8	8	8
8	8	x	x	x	8	8	8	8	8	8	8	8	8	8	8	8	8	8	8	8	8

Clothes Closet

Refer to the Word Bank and write the Spanish word for each item of clothing pictured.

Word Bank			
vestido	calcetines	botas	zapatos
sombrero	cinturón	falda	chaqueta
guantes	pantalones cortos	pantalones	camisa

shirt		pants	
shorts		hat	
socks		skirt	
shoes		belt	
boots		dress	
gloves		jacket	

Dressing Up

Write the Spanish word for each clue in the crossword puzzle.

Across

1. shoes
4. socks
7. dress
8. gloves
9. hat
10. shirt

Word Bank

cinturón	botas	camisa
guantes	calcetines	sombrero
chaqueta	falda	zapatos
pantalones	vestido	

Down

2. pants
3. skirt
4. jacket
5. belt
6. boots

Matching Clothes

At the bottom of each picture, write the English word that matches the Spanish and the pictures. Write the Spanish words next to the English at the bottom of the page.

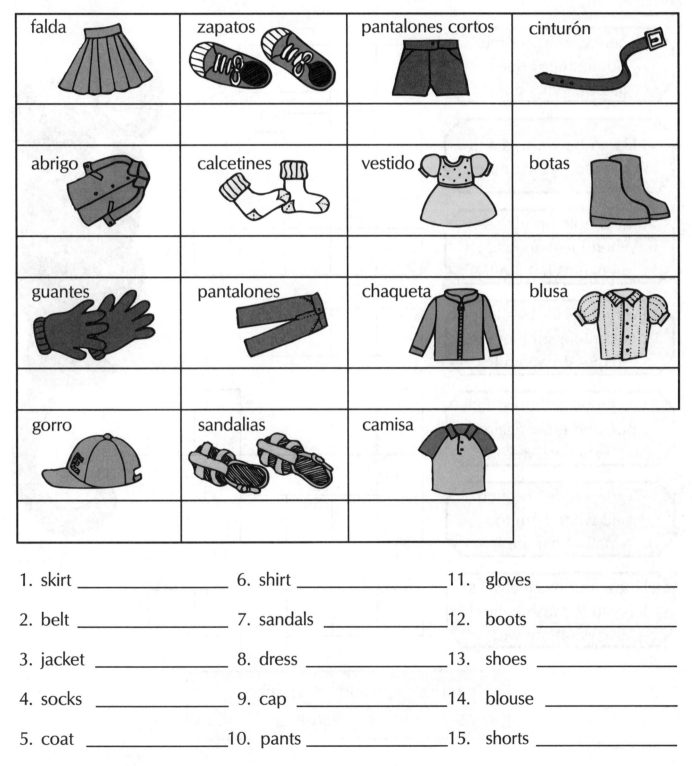

1. skirt _____
2. belt _____
3. jacket _____
4. socks _____
5. coat _____

6. shirt _____
7. sandals _____
8. dress _____
9. cap _____
10. pants _____

11. gloves _____
12. boots _____
13. shoes _____
14. blouse _____
15. shorts _____

Face Riddles

Can you guess the answers to the following riddles? Use the size and shape of the letter blocks to write the Spanish word. The answers at the bottom will help you.

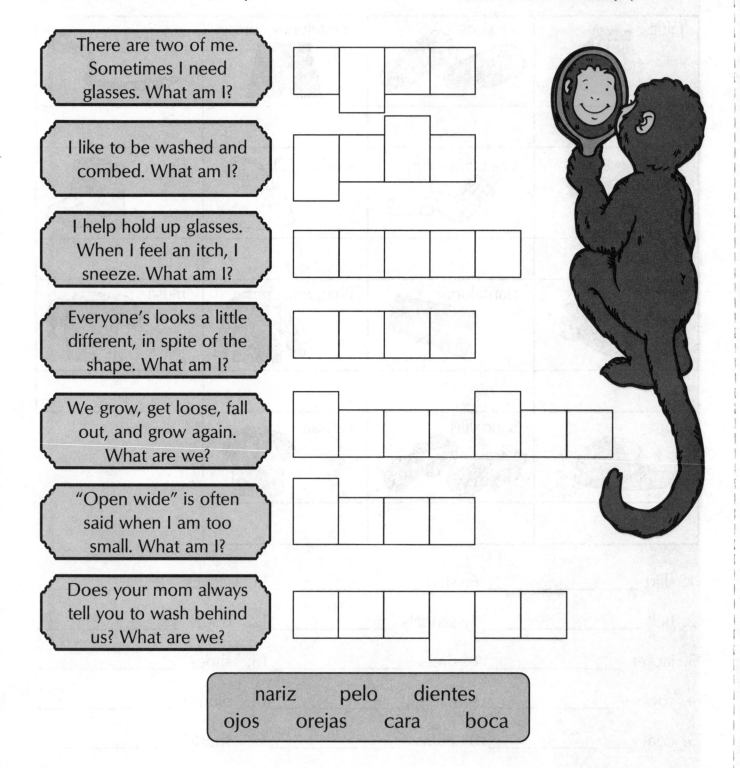

There are two of me. Sometimes I need glasses. What am I?

I like to be washed and combed. What am I?

I help hold up glasses. When I feel an itch, I sneeze. What am I?

Everyone's looks a little different, in spite of the shape. What am I?

We grow, get loose, fall out, and grow again. What are we?

"Open wide" is often said when I am too small. What am I?

Does your mom always tell you to wash behind us? What are we?

nariz   pelo   dientes
ojos   orejas   cara   boca

A Blank Face

Fill in the blanks with the missing letters. Use the Spanish words below to help you.

| nariz | pelo | dientes | ojos | orejas | cara | boca |

Which word didn't you use? _____

Color each block that has a letter k inside. Do not color the blocks with numbers.
What hidden word did you find? _____

k	5	5	5	5	5	5	5	5	5	5	5	5	5	5	5
k	5	5	5	5	5	5	5	5	5	5	5	5	5	5	5
k	5	5	5	5	5	5	5	5	5	5	5	5	5	5	5
k	k	k	5	k	k	k	5	k	k	k	5	k	k	k	5
k	5	k	5	k	5	k	5	k	5	5	5	k	5	k	5
k	5	k	5	k	5	k	5	k	5	5	5	k	5	k	5
k	k	k	5	k	k	k	5	k	k	k	5	k	k	k	k

How Are You?

Label each facial feature with a Spanish word from the Word Bank.

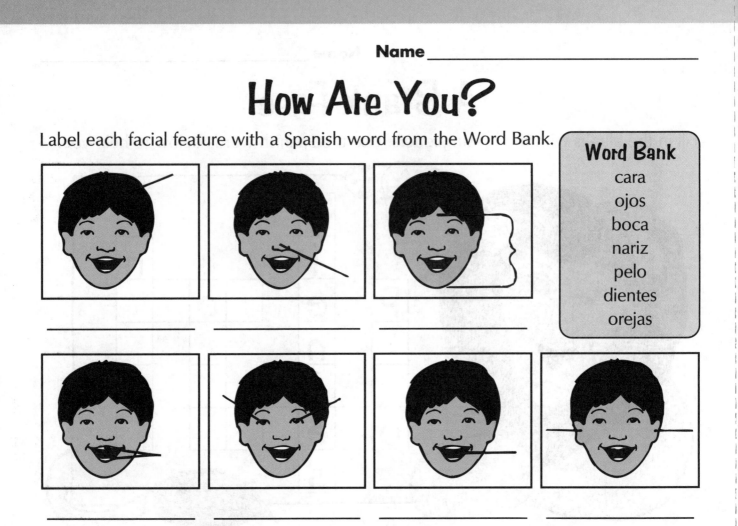

Word Bank
cara
ojos
boca
nariz
pelo
dientes
orejas

Copy the Spanish word that matches each face pictured.

Happy Faces

Write the Spanish for the clue words in the crossword puzzle.

Across

1. sad
3. nose
5. eyes
6. thinking
8. face
11. smiling
13. crying

Down

2. angry
4. happy
7. teeth
9. ears
10. mouth
12. hair

Word Bank

llorando	orejas	sonriendo	ojos
pelo	nariz	triste	cara
dientes	alegre	enojado	boca
pensando			

Matching Family

Cut out a picture of a family out of a magazine. Glue each picture next to the correct word.

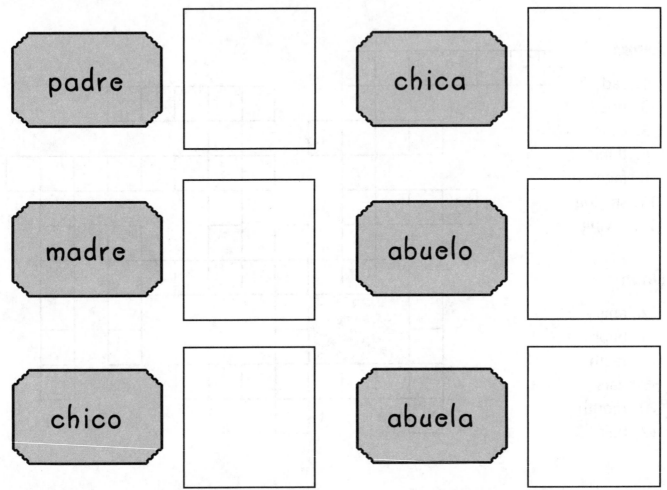

Try this: Color each block with a letter inside. Do not color the blocks with numbers.

What hidden word did you find? _____

2	2	2	2	2	2	2	2	2	2	2	2	2	m	2	2	2	2	2	2	2	2
2	2	2	2	2	2	2	2	2	2	2	2	2	m	2	2	2	2	2	2	2	2
m	m	m	m	m	2	m	m	m	2	2	m	m	m	2	m	m	m	2	m	m	m
m	2	m	2	m	2	m	2	m	2	2	m	2	m	2	m	2	m	2	m	2	m
m	2	m	2	m	2	m	2	m	2	2	m	2	m	2	m	2	2	2	m	m	m
m	2	m	2	m	2	m	2	m	2	2	m	2	m	2	m	2	2	2	m	2	2
m	2	m	2	m	2	m	m	m	m	2	m	m	m	2	m	2	2	2	m	m	m

Name _____

Family Ties

In each box, copy the Spanish word for family members.

la familia	family
el padre	father
la madre	mother
el hijo	son
la hija	daughter
los primos	cousins

el hermano	brother
la hermana	sister
el tío	uncle
la tía	aunt
el abuelo	grandfather
la abuela	grandmother

Write the Spanish words from above next to the English words.

sister _____   family _____   father _____

grandfather _____   cousins _____   mother _____

grandmother _____   brother _____   daughter _____

uncle _____   aunt _____   son _____

My Family

Write the Spanish word for each clue in the crossword puzzle.

Across

2. son
3. aunt
5. sister
7. grandmother
8. brother
10. cousins

Down

1. mother
2. daughter
4. family
6. grandfather
9. uncle
10. father

Word Bank

familia	hermano	hijo	tía
primos	madre	tío	abuelo
padre	hermana	hija	abuela

Family Tree

Refer to the Word Bank to write the Spanish word that matches each picture.

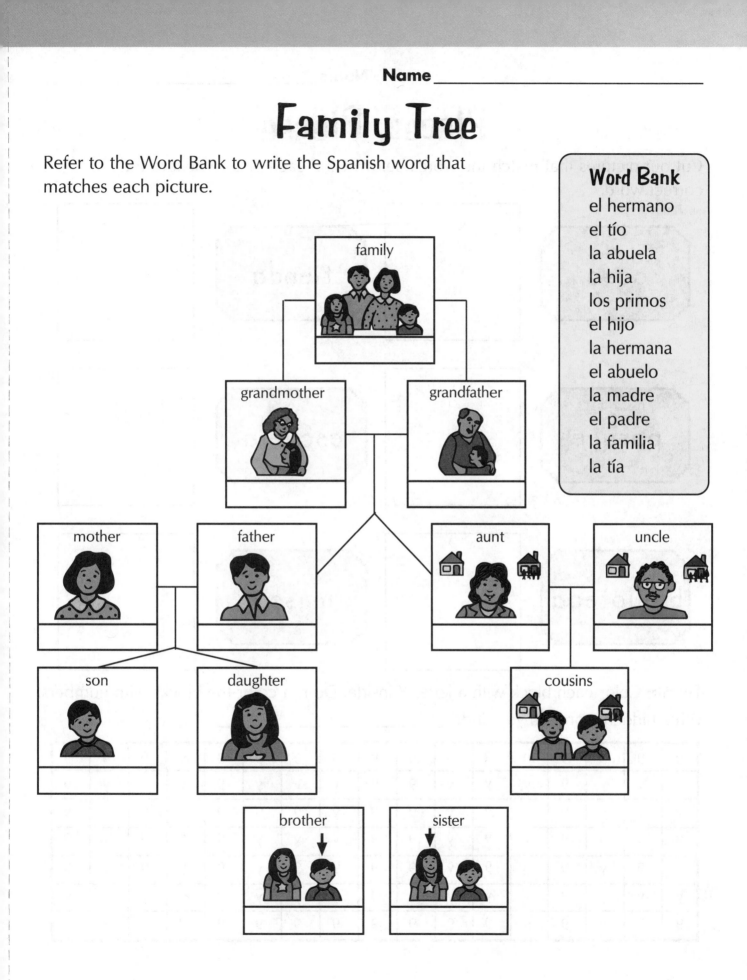

Word Bank

el hermano
el tío
la abuela
la hija
los primos
el hijo
la hermana
el abuelo
la madre
el padre
la familia
la tía

family

grandmother

grandfather

mother

father

aunt

uncle

son

daughter

cousins

brother

sister

Places, Please

Cut out pictures that match the words below. Glue each picture next to the correct word.

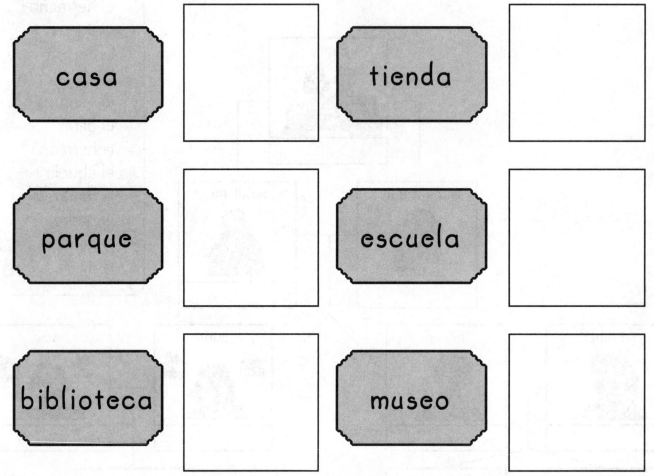

casa

tienda

parque

escuela

biblioteca

museo

Try this: Color each block with a letter Y inside. Do not color the blocks with numbers. What hidden word did you find? _____

9	9	9	9	9	9	9	9	9	9	9	9	9	9	9	9
y	y	y	9	y	y	y	9	9	y	y	y	9	y	y	y	9
y	9	y	9	y	9	y	9	9	y	9	9	9	y	9	y	9
y	9	9	9	y	9	y	9	9	y	y	y	9	y	9	y	9
y	9	y	9	y	9	y	9	9	9	9	y	9	y	9	y	9
y	y	y	9	y	y	y	y	9	y	y	y	9	y	y	y	y
9	9	9	9	9	9	9	9	9	9	9	9	9	9	9	9

A Place for Riddles

Answer the riddles. Use the size and shape of the letter blocks to write the Spanish words. The answers at the bottom of the page will help you.

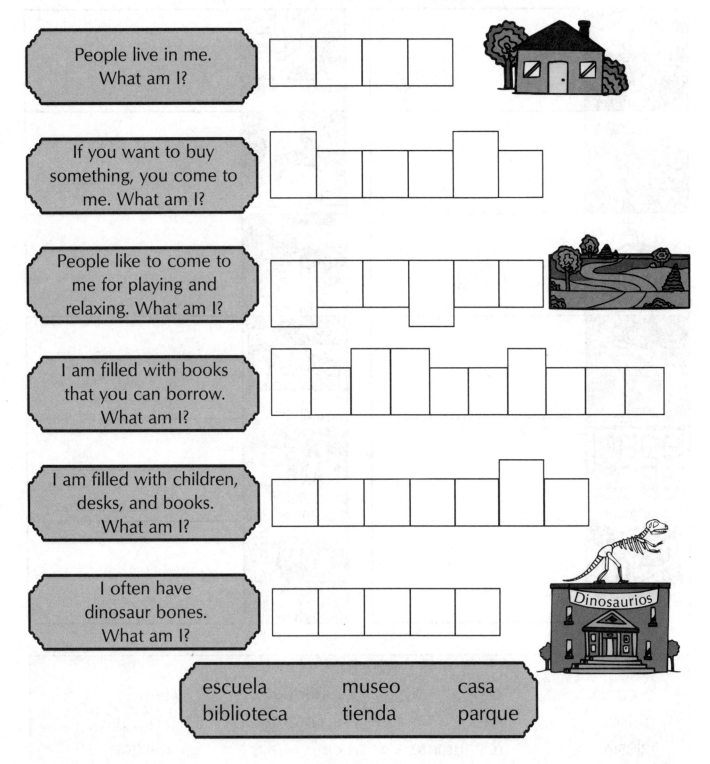

People live in me. What am I?

If you want to buy something, you come to me. What am I?

People like to come to me for playing and relaxing. What am I?

I am filled with books that you can borrow. What am I?

I am filled with children, desks, and books. What am I?

I often have dinosaur bones. What am I?

Dinosaurios

escuela   museo   casa
biblioteca   tienda   parque

Where Am I?

Refer to the Word Bank and write the Spanish for each place in the community pictured.

movie theater		museum	
farm		zoo	
church		library	
park		store	
apartment		house	
restaurant		school	

Word Bank

escuela	granja	biblioteca	tienda
museo	casa	apartamento	zoológico
iglesia	restaurante	cine	parque

Fitting In

Write the Spanish words from the Word Bank in these word blocks. Write the English meanings below the blocks.

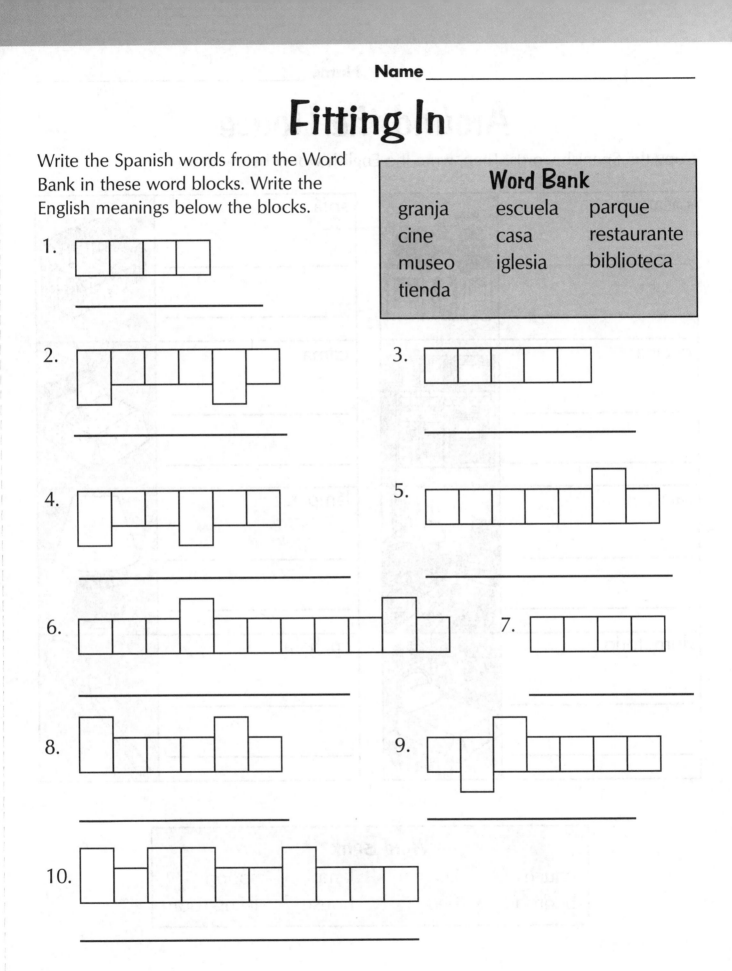

1.

2.

3.

4.

5.

6.

7.

8.

9.

10.

Around the House

Copy the Spanish words. Then, write the English words below them.

casa
_____
_____

sofá
_____
_____

cocina
_____
_____

cama
_____
_____

sala
_____
_____

lámpara
_____
_____

dormitorio
_____
_____

cuchara
_____
_____

Word Bank

couch	kitchen	lamp	spoon
bedroom	bed	house	living room

Around the Block

Write the Spanish words from the Word Bank that fit in these word blocks. Write the English below the blocks.

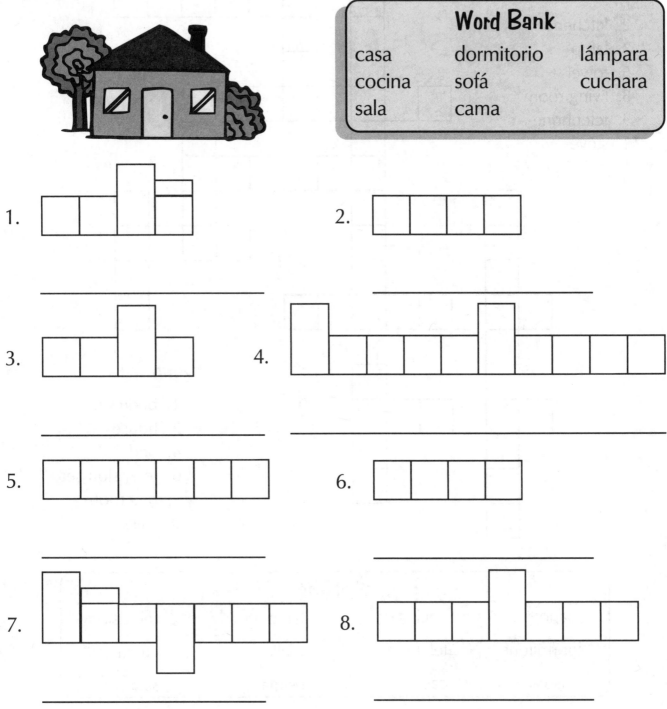

Word Bank

casa	dormitorio	lámpara
cocina	sofá	cuchara
sala	cama	

1.

2.

3.

4.

5.

6.

7.

8.

57 *Spanish: Grade 3*

Around the House

Write the Spanish words for the clue words in the crossword puzzle.

Across

2. kitchen
3. lamp
5. towel
8. living room
9. telephone
11. stove

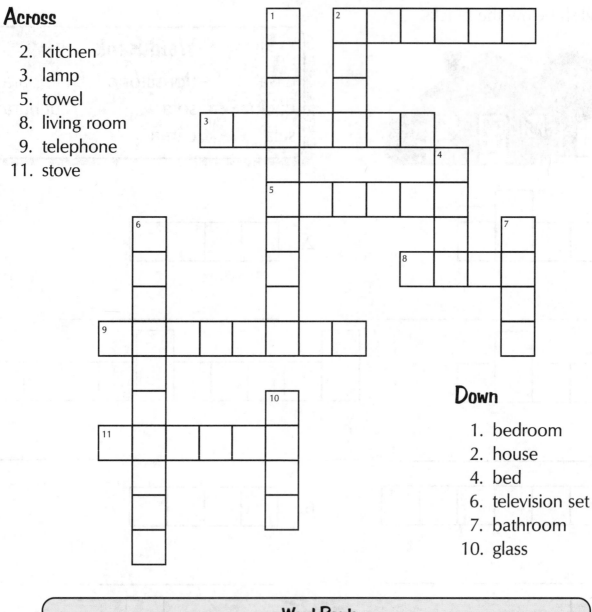

Down

1. bedroom
2. house
4. bed
6. television set
7. bathroom
10. glass

Word Bank

baño	cocina	lámpara	televisión
dormitorio	teléfono	toalla	cama
vaso	casa	estufa	sala

Match Words and Pictures

Cut out pictures from a magazine and glue each picture next to the correct word.

silla

borrador

mesa

lápiz

tijeras

libro

59

Spanish: Grade 3

Use the Clues

Use the clues and the words at the bottom of the page. Do not use any answer more than once.

1. Both words begin with the letter *p*. You write <u>with</u> one and write <u>on</u> one. What are they?

_____   _____

2. You can sit at either one of these when you need to write.

_____   _____

3. You could exit through either one of these in case of fire.

_____   _____

4. Both words end with the letter *o*. They both have pages.

_____   _____

5. These two words go together because one is on the end of the other.

_____   _____

6. Both words have an *i* as their second letter. One is used for cutting and the other is used for sitting.

_____   _____

silla	mesa	tijeras	libro	borrador	ventana
puerta	lápiz	cuaderno	papel	escritorio	pluma

Around the Room

In each box, copy the Spanish word for the classroom object pictured.

silla		mesa	
puerta		pluma	
ventana		borrador	
lápiz		cuaderno	
papel		libro	
escritorio		tijeras	

Write the Spanish words from above next to the English words.

window _____ chair _____ table _____

eraser _____ scissors _____ door _____

desk _____ pen _____ notebook _____

paper _____ book _____ pencil _____

61 *Spanish: Grade 3*

A Fitting Design

Write the Spanish words from the Word Bank that fit in these word blocks. Write the English meanings below the blocks.

Word Bank

ventana	papel	pluma	puerta
borrador	silla	libro	cuaderno
escritorio	tijeras	mesa	lápiz

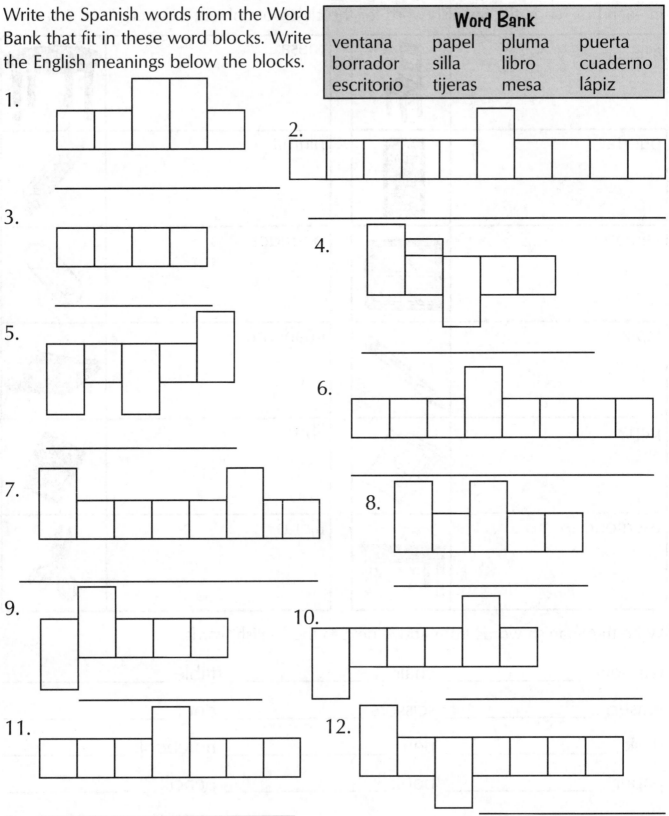

1.

2.

3.

4.

5.

6.

7.

8.

9.

10.

11.

12.

Classroom Clutter

Draw a picture to illustrate each of the Spanish words. Refer to the Word Bank at the bottom of the page to help you.

silla	ventana
mesa	puerta
tijeras	papel
libro	cuaderno
lápiz	escritorio
borrador	pluma

Word Bank

eraser	door	scissors	pen	window	paper
chair	notebook	pencil	desk	book	table

Spanish: Grade 3

Show and Tell

Write the Spanish for each clue in the crossword puzzle.

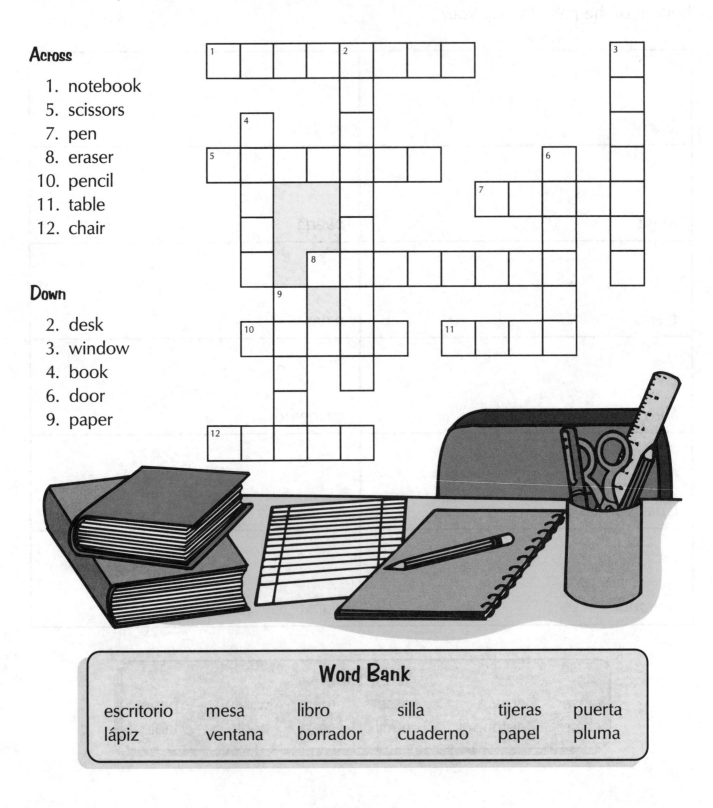

Across

1. notebook
5. scissors
7. pen
8. eraser
10. pencil
11. table
12. chair

Down

2. desk
3. window
4. book
6. door
9. paper

Word Bank

escritorio   mesa   libro   silla   tijeras   puerta
lápiz   ventana   borrador   cuaderno   papel   pluma

Songs and Chants

Food Song

(to the tune of "She'll Be Coming 'Round the Mountain")

Queso is cheese, yum, yum, yum. (clap, clap)
Leche is milk, yum, yum, yum. (clap, clap)
Papa is potato.
Jugo is juice.
Pan is bread, yum, yum, yum! (clap, clap)

Pollo is chicken, yum, yum, yum. (clap, clap)
Ensalada is salad, yum, yum, yum. (clap, clap)
Queso, leche, papa,
jugo, pan, pollo, ensalada,
yum, yum, yum, yum, yum! (clap, clap)

Community Song

(to the tune of "Here We Go 'Round the Mulberry Bush")

Escuela is school,   museo museum;
casa is house,   tienda is store;
biblioteca is library;   parque is the park for me!

       Spanish: Grade 3

Songs

¡Hola, chicos!

(to the tune of "Goodnight Ladies")

¡Hola, chico! ¡Hola, chica!
¡Hola, chicos! ¿Cómo están hoy?
¡Hola, chico! ¡Hola, chica!
¡Hola, chicos! ¿Cómo están hoy?

Los días de la semana

(to the tune of "Clementine")

Domingo, lunes,
martes, miércoles,
jueves, viernes, sábado,
domingo, lunes,
martes, miércoles,
jueves, viernes, sábado. (Repitan)

66

Learning Cards

Cut out the learning cards. Practice saying the Spanish words using the learning cards.

levántense	**cierren**
siéntense	**cállensen**
abran	**póngansen**

Learning Cards

close	**stand up**
be quiet	**sit down**
line up	**open**

68

Learning Cards

Cut out the learning cards. Practice saying the Spanish words using the learning cards.

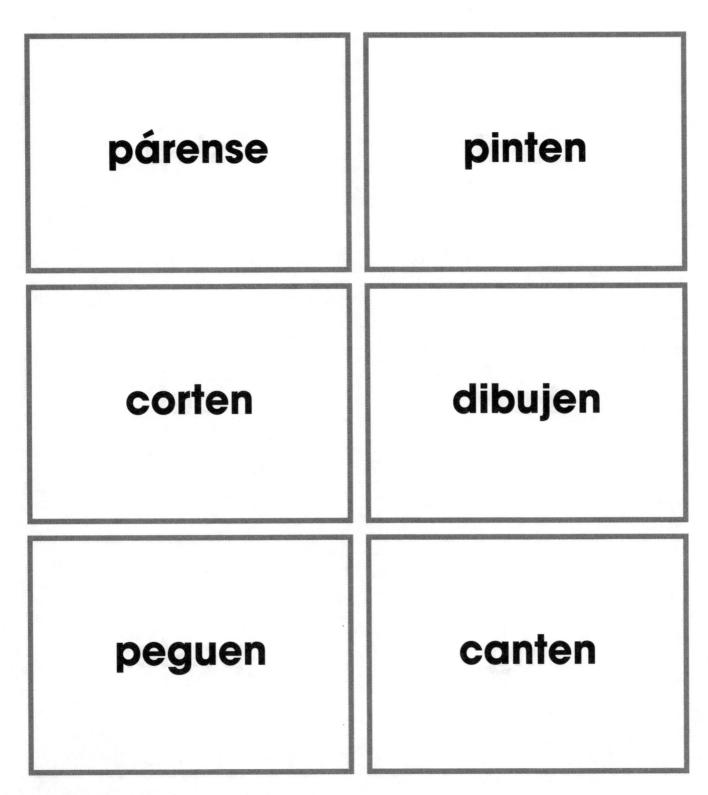

párense	**pinten**
corten	**dibujen**
peguen	**canten**

Learning Cards

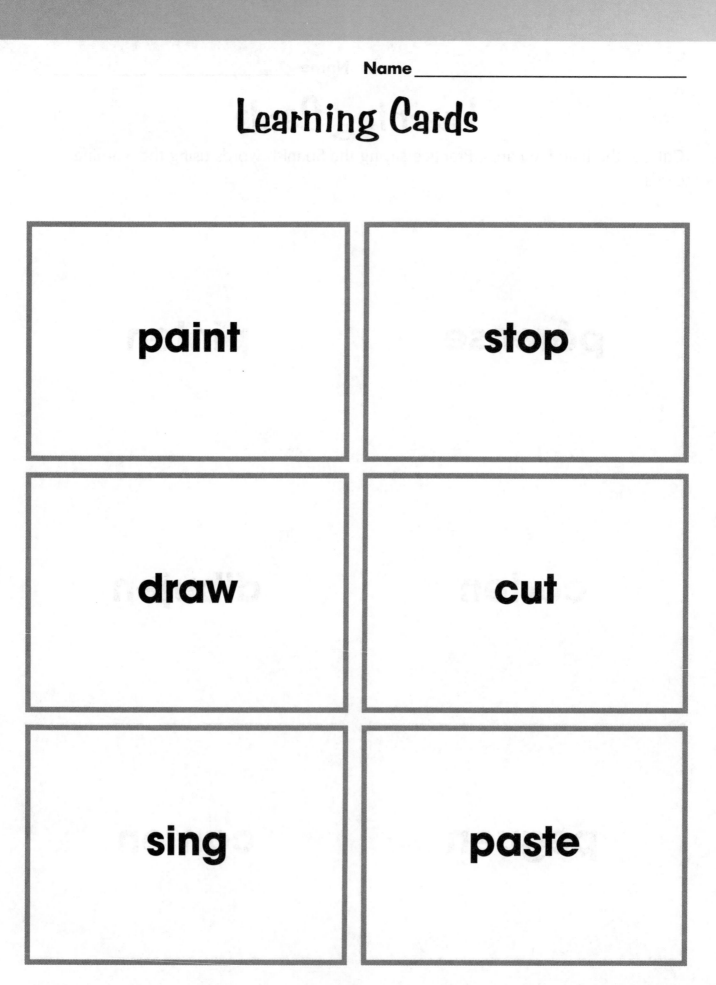

paint	stop
draw	cut
sing	paste

Numbers Crossword

Use the words at the bottom to help you with this crossword puzzle. Write the Spanish number words in the puzzle spaces. Follow the English clues.

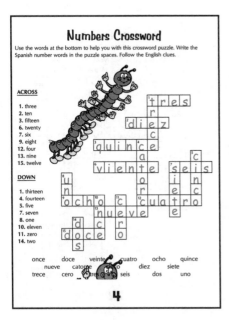

ACROSS

1. three
2. ten
3. fifteen
6. twenty
7. six
9. eight
12. four
13. nine
15. twelve

DOWN

1. thirteen
4. fourteen
5. five
7. seven
8. one
10. eleven
11. zero
14. two

Crossword answers:
- 1 across: tres
- 2 across: diez
- 3 across: quince
- 6 across: viente
- 7 across: seis
- 4 down: ocho
- cuatro
- nueve
- doce

once   doce   veinte   cuatro   ocho   quince
nueve   catorce   cinco   diez   siete
trece   cero   tres   seis   dos   uno

4

Numbers

After each numeral, write the number word in Spanish. Refer to the words below to help you.

Word Bank

veinte	cuatro	nueve	diez	diecisiete	quince
doce	once	trece	siete	uno	tres
catorce	dos	cero	ocho	cinco	dieciséis
diecinueve		dieciocho		seis	

0	cero	11	once
1	uno	12	dos
2	dos	13	trece
3	tres	14	catorce
4	cuatro	15	quince
5	cinco	16	dieciséis
6	seis	17	diecisiete
7	siete	18	dieciocho
8	ocho	19	diecinueve
9	nueve	20	veinte
10	diez		

5

Numbers Illustration

Write the number. Draw that many things in the box. The first one is done for you.

★★★★ ★★★★		
ocho means __8__	cinco means __5__	diecisiete means __17__
Pictures Will Vary.		
doce means __12__	uno means __1__	dos means __2__
catorce means __14__	nueve means __9__	veinte means __20__
siete means __7__	cuatro means __4__	quince means __15__

6

Who Is It?

Write the names of people you may know that fit each description below.

tú–informal or familiar form of you

someone you refer to by first name	
your sister or brother (or cousin)	
a classmate	Answers Will Vary.
a close friend	
a child younger than yourself	

usted–formal or polite form of you

someone with a title	
an older person	
a stranger	Answers Will Vary.
a person of authority	

How would you speak to each person below? Write *tú* or *usted* after each person named.

1. Dr. Hackett __usted__
2. Susana __tú__
3. a four-year-old __tú__
4. your grandfather __usted__
5. the governor __usted__
6. your best friend __tú__
7. your sister __tú__
8. the principal __usted__
9. a classmate __tú__
10. a stranger __usted__

7

Masculine and Feminine

All Spanish nouns and adjectives have gender. This means they are either masculine or feminine. Here are two basic rules to help determine the gender of words. There are other rules for gender which you will learn as you study more Spanish.

1. Spanish words ending in -o are usually masculine.
2. Spanish words ending in -a are usually feminine.

Write the following words in the charts to determine their gender. Write the English meanings to the right. Use a Spanish-English dictionary if you need help.

maestra	libro	escritorio	negro	abrigo	sopa	tienda
amigo	ventana	pluma	maestro	vestido	fruta	museo
silla	puerta	anaranjado	amiga	camisa	queso	casa
rojo	cuaderno	blanco	falda	chaqueta		

Masculine

words ending in -o	meaning of the word
amigo	friend (male)
rojo	red
libro	book
cuaderno	notebook
escriturio	desk
anaranjado	orange
museo	museum
blanco	white
negro	black
maestro	teacher (male)
abrigo	coat
vestido	dress
queso	cheese

Feminine

words ending in -a	meaning of the word
maestra	teacher (female)
silla	chair
ventana	window
puerta	door
pluma	pen
amiga	friend (female)
falda	skirt
camisa	shirt
chaqueta	jacket
sopa	soup
fruta	fruit
tienda	store
casa	house

8

It's a Small World

In Spanish, there are four ways to say "the"—*el*, *la*, *los*, and *las*. The definite article (the) agrees with its noun in gender (masculine or feminine) and number (singular or plural).

Masculine singular nouns go with *el*. Feminine singular nouns go with *la*.

Examples: *el libro* (the book)   *el papel* (the paper)
la silla (the chair)   *la regla* (the ruler)

Masculine plural nouns go with *los*. Feminine plural nouns go with *las*.

Examples: *los libros* (the books)   *los papeles* (the papers)
las sillas (the chairs)   *las reglas* (the rulers)

Refer to the Word Bank to complete the chart. Write the singular and plural forms and the correct definite articles. The first ones have been done for you.

Word Bank: cuaderno   mesa   pluma   oso   falda   papel   gato   bota   silla   libro

English	Masculine Singular	Masculine Plural
the book	el libro	los libros
the paper	el papel	los papeles
the notebook	el cuaderno	los cuadernos
the cat	el gato	los gatos
the bear	el oso	los osos

English	Feminine Singular	Feminine Plural
the chair	la silla	las sillas
the table	la mesa	las mesas
the boot	la bota	la botas
the skirt	la falda	las faldas
the pen	la pluma	las plumas

9

Pretty Colors

Adjectives are words that tell about or describe nouns. Color each box as indicated in Spanish. Use a Spanish-English dictionary if you need help.

rojo	azul	verde	anaranjado	morado
amarillo	café	negro	blanco	rosado

Here are some new adjectives. Copy the Spanish adjectives in the boxes. Write the Spanish words next to the English at the bottom of the page.

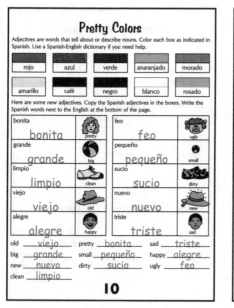

bonita	feo
bonita (pretty)	feo (ugly)
grande	pequeño
grande (big)	pequeño (small)
limpio	sucio
limpio (clean)	sucio (dirty)
viejo	nuevo
viejo (old)	nuevo (new)
alegre	triste
alegre (happy)	triste (sad)

old _viejo_   pretty _bonita_   sad _triste_
big _grande_   small _pequeño_   happy _alegre_
new _nuevo_   dirty _sucio_   ugly _feo_
clean _limpio_

10

Words to Describe

Descriptive adjectives are words that describe nouns. Refer to the Word Bank to write the Spanish adjective that describes each picture.

Word Bank
alegre grande nuevo pequeño feo rico
limpio sucio bonita triste viejo pobre
alto bajo abierto cerrado

large	new	ugly	happy
grande	nuevo	feo	alegre
old	sad	small	clean
viejo	triste	pequeño	limpio
pretty	dirty	tall	open
bonita	sucio	alto	abierto
rich	short	closed	poor
rico	bajo	cerrado	pobre

11

Words to Describe

Write the Spanish words for the clue words in the crossword puzzle.

Across
3. poor
7. open
9. tall
11. clean
12. dirty
13. new

Down
1. ugly
2. closed
4. happy
5. pretty
6. large
8. old
10. sad

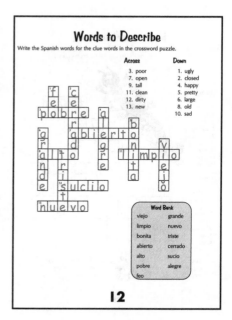

Word Bank
viejo · grande
limpio · nuevo
bonita · triste
abierto · cerrado
alto · sucio
pobre · alegre
feo

12

Action Words

In each box, copy the Spanish action verbs. Then, write the English word below it.

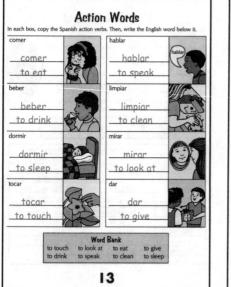

comer	hablar
comer	hablar
to eat	to speak
beber	limpiar
beber	limpiar
to drink	to clean
dormir	mirar
dormir	mirar
to sleep	to look at
tocar	dar
tocar	dar
to touch	to give

Word Bank
| to touch | to look at | to eat | to give |
| to drink | to speak | to clean | to sleep |

13

Action Figures

Write the Spanish words from the Word Bank that fit in these word blocks. Write the English below the blocks.

Word Bank
mirar limpiar tocar beber
hablar comer dar dormir

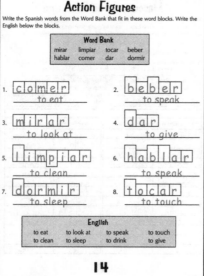

1. comer — to eat
2. beber — to speak
3. mirar — to look at
4. dar — to give
5. limpiar — to clean
6. hablar — to speak
7. dormir — to sleep
8. tocar — to touch

English
| to eat | to look at | to speak | to touch |
| to clean | to sleep | to drink | to give |

14

Greetings Paste Up

Cut out a picture from a magazine that shows the meaning of each greeting and glue it next to the correct word or words.

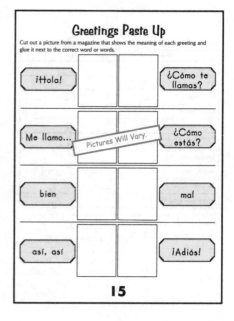

¡Hola!   ¿Cómo te llamas?

Me llamo...   *Pictures Will Vary.*   ¿Cómo estás?

bien   mal

así, así   ¡Adiós!

15

What's Your Name?

Word Bank

I'm so-so.	What's your name?	I'm well/fine.
I'm ___ years old.	I'm not doing well.	My name is ___.
I'm so-so.	How are you?	How old are you?

Refer to the Word Bank to translate the Spanish questions and answers into English.

1. ¿Cómo te llamas? _What is your name?_
   Me llamo _My name is_
2. ¿Cómo estás? _How are you?_
   Estoy bien/mal/así así. _I'm fine. I'm not well. I'm so-so._
3. ¿Cuántos años tienes? _How old are you?_
   Tengo ___ años. _I am ___ years old._

Word Bank

hello	please	friend	yes
no	thank you	goodbye	See you later!

Write the English meaning after the Spanish word.

4. hola _hello_
5. amigo, amiga _friend (m/f)_
6. sí _yes_
7. no _no_
8. por favor _please_
9. gracias _thank you_
10. ¡Hasta luego! _See you later!_
11. adiós _goodbye_

16

Word Blocks

Write the Spanish words from the Word Bank that fit in these word blocks. Don't forget the punctuation. Write the English meanings below the blocks.

1. hola — hello
2. por favor — please
3. no — no
4. ¡Hasta luego! — See you later!
5. ¿Cómo estás? — How are you?
6. ¿Cómo te llamas? — What is your name?
7. adiós — goodbye

Spanish Word Bank

por favor	adiós	Estoy bien.
hola	¡Hasta luego!	¿Cómo te llamas?
no	¿Cómo estás?	

8. Estoy bien. — I am fine.

17

Greetings

Write the English meaning of the Spanish words and phrases.

1. señor _Mr._
2. señora _Mrs._
3. señorita _Miss_
4. maestro _teacher (male)_
5. maestra _teacher (female)_
6. ¡Buenos días! _Good morning!_
7. ¡Buenas tardes! _Good afternoon!_
8. ¡Buenas noches! _Good night!_
9. Vamos a contar. _Let's count_

Word Bank

Mr.	Good night!	Good morning!
Good afternoon!	teacher (female)	teacher (male)
Miss	Let's count.	Mrs.

Draw a picture to show the time of day that you use each expression.

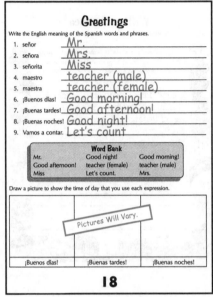

Pictures Will Vary.

¡Buenos días!	¡Buenas tardes!	¡Buenas noches!

18

Spanish Greetings

Write the Spanish word for each clue in the crossword puzzle.

Across
1. bad
4. good
7. teacher (male)
9. friend (female)
10. Mr.
11. Miss

Down
2. friend (male)
3. hello
5. thank you
6. goodbye
7. teacher (female)
8. Mrs.

Word Bank

amiga	mal
señora	señor
maestra	bien
adiós	hola
señorita	gracias
amigo	maestro

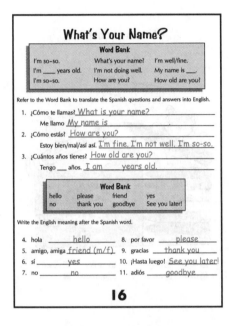

19

Yesterday and Today

Write the Spanish words for the days of the week. Remember, in Spanish-speaking countries, Monday is the first day of the week.

Word Bank

miércoles	jueves	sábado
viernes	lunes	martes
	domingo	

Monday	lunes
Tuesday	martes
Wednesday	miércoles
Thursday	jueves
Friday	viernes
Saturday	sábado
Sunday	domingo

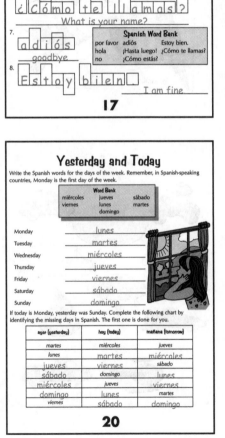

If today is Monday, yesterday was Sunday. Complete the following chart by identifying the missing days in Spanish. The first one is done for you.

ayer (yesterday)	hoy (today)	mañana (tomorrow)
martes	miércoles	jueves
lunes	martes	miércoles
jueves	viernes	sábado
sábado	domingo	lunes
miércoles	jueves	viernes
domingo	lunes	martes
viernes	sábado	domingo

20

Rain in April

Refer to the Word Bank to write the Spanish word for the given month. Then, in the box, draw a picture of something that happens in that month of the year. Remember that Spanish months do not begin with capital letters.

Word Bank

agosto	septiembre	noviembre	mayo
junio	enero	octubre	febrero
marzo	julio	diciembre	abril

January	enero	July	julio
February	febrero	August	agosto
March	marzo	September	septiembre
April	abril	October	octubre
May	mayo	November	noviembre
June	junio	December	diciembre

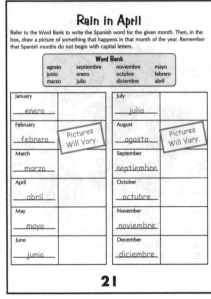

Pictures Will Vary. (February, August)

21

Spanish: Grade 3

Writing Practice

Copy the following paragraph in your best handwriting. Practice reading it out loud.

Hay doce meses en un año. Diciembre, enero y febrero son en el invierno. Marzo, abril y mayo son en la primavera. Junio, julio y agosto son en el verano. Septiembre, octubre y noviembre son en el otoño. ¿Cuál es tú favorito mes del año?

Hay doce meses en un año.
Diciembre, enero y febrero son
en el invierno. Marzo, abril y
mayo son en la primavera. Junio,
julio y agosto son en el verano.
Septiembre, octubre y
noviembre son en el otoño. ¿Cuál
es tú favorito mes del año?

22

Birds of Color

Color the birds according to the words listed.

azul
café
morado
rosado
rojo
verde
negro
amarillo
anaranjado

23

House of Colors

Color each crayon with the correct color for the Spanish word. Add something with your favorite color.

Pictures Will Vary.

azul
verde
amarillo
blanco
rojo
negro
rosado

rosado
negro
azul
rojo
amarillo
café
verde

☐ rojo ■ negro ☐ café ☐ rosado
■ azul ☐ amarillo ☐ blanco ■ verde

24

Color the Flowers

Color each flower with the correct color for the Spanish word.

morado
amarillo
rojo
café
rosado
anaranjado
azul
verde

■ azul ☐ café ☐ amarillo ☐ rosado
■ verde ☐ rojo ☐ morado ☐ anaranjado

25

Moving Colors

Color the pictures according to the words listed.

verde
rojo
anaranjado
blanco
rosado
amarillo
azul
café
morado

What is your favorite color? (Answer in Spanish.)   Answers Will Vary.

26

Color Crossword

Write the correct Spanish color words in the spaces. Follow the English color clues.

ACROSS
3. yellow
5. purple
6. black
8. white
10. pink

DOWN
1. blue
2. red
4. orange
7. green
9. brown

a z u l
r
a m a r i l l o o j
n o
m o r a d o
a
n e g r o
i
v b l a n c o
e a
r o s a d o f é
d
e

| blanco | rojo | anaranjado | verde | rosado |
| azul | morado | amarillo | café | negro |

27

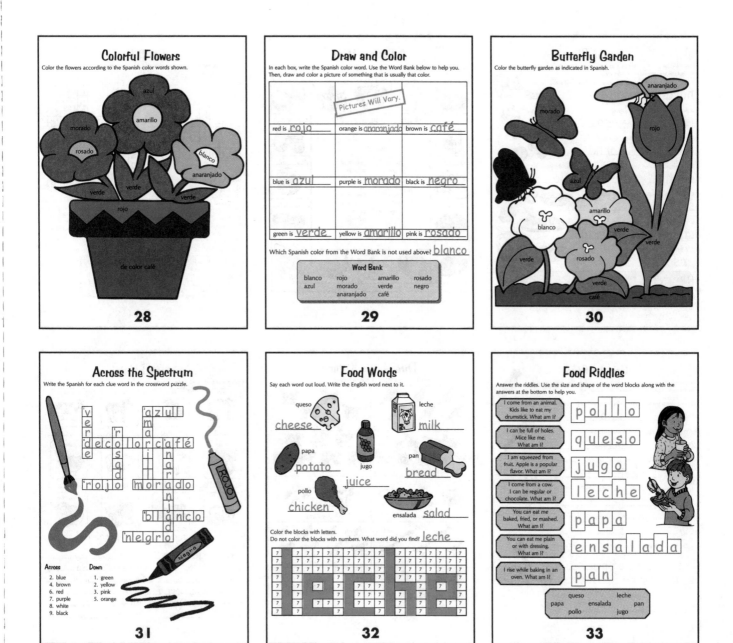

Colorful Flowers

Color the flowers according to the Spanish color words shown.

azul
amarillo
morado
rosado
blanco
anaranjado
verde
verde
verde
rojo
de color café

28

Draw and Color

In each box, write the Spanish color word. Use the Word Bank below to help you. Then, draw and color a picture of something that is usually that color.

Pictures Will Vary.

red is rojo	orange is anaranjado	brown is café
blue is azul	purple is morado	black is negro
green is verde	yellow is amarillo	pink is rosado

Which Spanish color from the Word Bank is not used above? blanco

Word Bank

blanco	rojo	amarillo	rosado
azul	morado	verde	negro
	anaranjado	café	

29

Butterfly Garden

Color the butterfly garden as indicated in Spanish.

anaranjado
morado
rojo
azul
amarillo
blanco
verde
verde
rosado
verde
café

30

Across the Spectrum

Write the Spanish for each clue word in the crossword puzzle.

azul
de color café
rojo morado
blanco
negro

Across
2. blue
4. brown
6. red
7. purple
8. white
9. black

Down
1. green
2. yellow
3. pink
5. orange

31

Food Words

Say each word out loud. Write the English word next to it.

queso — cheese
leche — milk
papa — potato
jugo — juice
pan — bread
pollo — chicken
ensalada — salad

Color the blocks with letters.
Do not color the blocks with numbers. What word did you find? leche

32

Food Riddles

Answer the riddles. Use the size and shape of the word blocks along with the answers at the bottom to help you.

I come from an animal. Kids like to eat my drumstick. What am I? — pollo

I can be full of holes. Mice like me. What am I? — queso

I am squeezed from fruit. Apple is a popular flavor. What am I? — jugo

I come from a cow. I can be regular or chocolate. What am I? — leche

You can eat me baked, fried, or mashed. What am I? — papa

You can eat me plain or with dressing. What am I? — ensalada

I rise while baking in an oven. What am I? — pan

queso   leche
papa   ensalada   pan
pollo   jugo

33

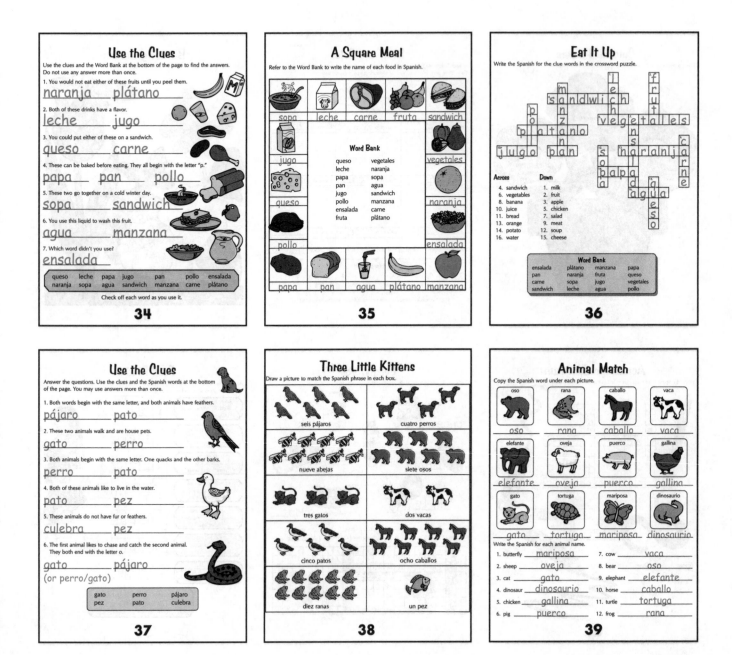

Use the Clues

Use the clues and the Word Bank at the bottom of the page to find the answers.
Do not use any answer more than once.

1. You would not eat either of these fruits until you peel them.
naranja   plátano

2. Both of these drinks have a flavor.
leche   jugo

3. You could put either of these on a sandwich.
queso   carne

4. These can be baked before eating. They all begin with the letter "p."
papa   pan   pollo

5. These two go together on a cold winter day.
sopa   sandwich

6. You use this liquid to wash this fruit.
agua   manzana

7. Which word didn't you use?
ensalada

| queso | leche | papa | jugo | pan | pollo | ensalada |
| naranja | sopa | agua | sandwich | manzana | carne | plátano |

Check off each word as you use it.

34

A Square Meal

Refer to the Word Bank to write the name of each food in Spanish.

sopa · leche · carne · fruta · sandwich
jugo · · · · vegetales
queso · · · · naranja
pollo · · · · ensalada
papa · pan · agua · plátano · manzana

Word Bank

queso	vegetales
leche	naranja
papa	sopa
pan	agua
jugo	sandwich
pollo	manzana
ensalada	carne
fruta	plátano

35

Eat It Up

Write the Spanish for the clue words in the crossword puzzle.

sandwich · fruta · vegetales · plátano · jugo · pan · naranja · sopa · papa · carne · agua · queso

Across
4. sandwich
6. vegetables
8. banana
10. juice
11. bread
13. orange
14. potato
16. water

Down
1. milk
2. fruit
3. apple
5. chicken
7. salad
9. meat
12. soup
15. cheese

Word Bank

ensalada	plátano	manzana	papa
pan	naranja	fruta	queso
carne	sopa	jugo	vegetales
sandwich	leche	agua	pollo

36

Use the Clues

Answer the questions. Use the clues and the Spanish words at the bottom
of the page. You may use answers more than once.

1. Both words begin with the same letter, and both animals have feathers.
pájaro   pato

2. These two animals walk and are house pets.
gato   perro

3. Both animals begin with the same letter. One quacks and the other barks.
perro   pato

4. Both of these animals like to live in the water.
pato   pez

5. These animals do not have fur or feathers.
culebra   pez

6. The first animal likes to chase and catch the second animal.
They both end with the letter o.
gato   pájaro
(or perro/gato)

| gato | perro | pájaro |
| pez | pato | culebra |

37

Three Little Kittens

Draw a picture to match the Spanish phrase in each box.

seis pájaros	cuatro perros
nueve abejas	siete osos
tres gatos	dos vacas
cinco patos	ocho caballos
diez ranas	un pez

38

Animal Match

Copy the Spanish word under each picture.

oso	rana	caballo	vaca
oso	rana	caballo	vaca
elefante	oveja	puerco	gallina
elefante	oveja	puerco	gallina
gato	tortuga	mariposa	dinosaurio
gato	tortuga	mariposa	dinosaurio

Write the Spanish for each animal name.

1. butterfly   mariposa   7. cow   vaca
2. sheep   oveja   8. bear   oso
3. cat   gato   9. elephant   elefante
4. dinosaur   dinosaurio   10. horse   caballo
5. chicken   gallina   11. turtle   tortuga
6. pig   puerco   12. frog   rana

39

Clothes to Color

Cut out pictures and glue them next to the correct words.

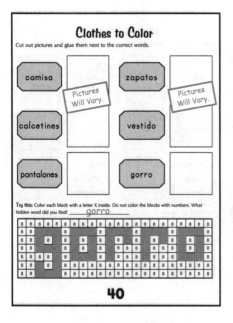

camisa	Pictures Will Vary.	zapatos	Pictures Will Vary.
calcetines		vestido	
pantalones		gorro	

Try this: Color each block with a letter X inside. Do not color the blocks with numbers. What hidden word did you find? __gorro__

40

Clothes Closet

Refer to the Word Bank and write the Spanish word for each item of clothing pictured.

Word Bank

vestido calcetines botas zapatos
sombrero cinturón falda chaqueta
guantes pantalones cortos pantalones camisa

shirt	camisa	pants	pantalones
shorts	pantalones cortos	hat	sombrero
socks	calcetines	skirt	falda
shoes	zapatos	belt	cinturón
boots	botas	dress	vestido
gloves	guantes	jacket	chaqueta

41

Dressing Up

Write the Spanish word for each clue in the crossword puzzle.

Across
1. shoes
4. socks
7. dress
8. gloves
9. hat
10. shirt

Down
2. pants
3. skirt
4. jacket
5. belt
6. boots

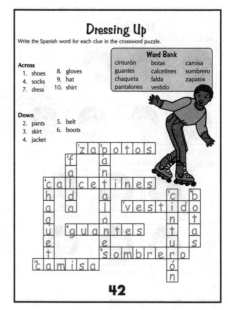

Word Bank

cinturón botas camisa
guantes calcetines sombrero
chaqueta falda zapatos
pantalones vestido

Crossword answers: zapatos, falda, calcetines, vestido, guantes, sombrero, cinturón, camisa

42

Matching Clothes

At the bottom of each picture, write the English word that matches the Spanish and the pictures. Write the Spanish words next to the English at the bottom of the page.

falda	zapatos	pantalones cortos	cinturón
skirt	shoes	shorts	belt
abrigo	calcetines	vestido	botas
coat	socks	dress	boots
guantes	pantalones	chaqueta	blusa
gloves	pants	jacket	blouse
gorro	sandalias	camisa	
cap	sandals	shirt	

1. skirt __falda__
2. belt __cinturón__
3. jacket __chaqueta__
4. socks __calcetines__
5. coat __abrigo__
6. shirt __camisa__
7. sandals __sandalias__
8. dress __vestido__
9. cap __gorro__
10. pants __pantalones__
11. gloves __guantes__
12. boots __botas__
13. shoes __zapatos__
14. blouse __blusa__
15. shorts __pantalones cortos__

43

Face Riddles

Can you guess the answers to the following riddles? Use the size and shape of the letter blocks to write the Spanish word. The answers at the bottom will help you.

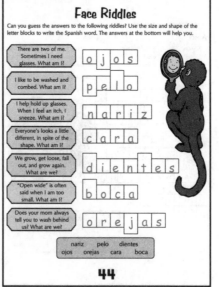

There are two of me. Sometimes I need glasses. What am I? — o j o s

I like to be washed and combed. What am I? — p e l o

I help hold up glasses. When I feel an itch, I sneeze. What am I? — n a r i z

Everyone's looks a little different, in spite of the shape. What am I? — c a r a

We grow, get loose, fall out, and grow again. What are we? — d i e n t e s

"Open wide" is often said when I am too small. What am I? — b o c a

Does your mom always tell you to wash behind us? What are we? — o r e j a s

nariz   pelo   dientes
ojos   orejas   cara   boca

44

A Blank Face

Fill in the blanks with the missing letters. Use the Spanish words below to help you.

nariz   pelo   dientes   ojos   orejas   cara   boca

Which word didn't you use? __cara__

Color each block that has a letter k inside. Do not color the blocks with numbers. What hidden word did you find? __boca__

45

Spanish: Grade 3

How Are You?

Label each facial feature with a Spanish word from the Word Bank.

Word Bank
cara
ojos
boca
nariz
pelo
dientes
orejas

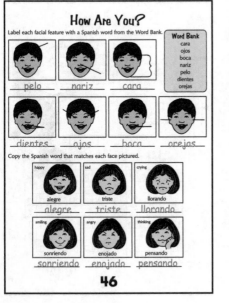

pelo   nariz   cara

dientes   ojos   boca   orejas

Copy the Spanish word that matches each face pictured.

happy	sad	crying
alegre	triste	llorando
alegre	triste	llorando

smiling	angry	thinking
sonriendo	enojado	pensando
sonriendo	enojado	pensando

46

Happy Faces

Write the Spanish for the clue words in the crossword puzzle.

Across
1. sad
3. nose
5. eyes
6. thinking
8. face
11. smiling
13. crying

Down
2. angry
4. happy
7. teeth
9. ears
10. mouth
12. hair

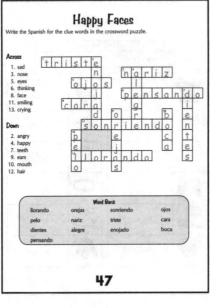

Word Bank

llorando	orejas	sonriendo	ojos
pelo	nariz	triste	cara
dientes	alegre	enojado	boca
pensando			

47

Matching Family

Cut out a picture of a family out of a magazine. Glue each picture next to the correct word.

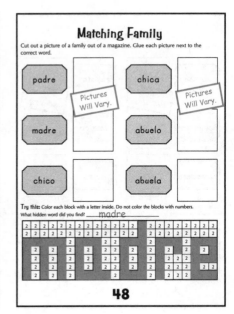

padre   chica
Pictures Will Vary.   *Pictures Will Vary.*

madre   abuelo

chico   abuela

Try this: Color each block with a letter inside. Do not color the blocks with numbers. What hidden word did you find? __madre__

48

Family Ties

In each box, copy the Spanish word for family members.

la familia		el hermano	
la familia	family	el hermano	brother
el padre		la hermana	
el padre	father	la hermana	sister
la madre		el tío	
la madre	mother	el tío	uncle
el hijo		la tía	
el hijo	son	la tía	aunt
la hija		el abuelo	
la hija	daughter	el abuelo	grandfather
los primos		la abuela	
los primos	cousins	la abuela	grandmother

Write the Spanish words from above next to the English words.

sister la hermana   family la familia   father el padre
grandfather el abuelo   cousins los primos   mother la madre
grandmother la abuela   brother el hermano   daughter la hija
uncle el tío   aunt la tía   son el hijo

49

My Family

Write the Spanish word for each clue in the crossword puzzle.

Across
2. son
3. aunt
5. sister
7. grandmother
8. brother
10. cousins

Down
1. mother
2. daughter
4. family
6. grandfather
9. uncle
10. father

Word Bank

familia	hermano	hijo	tía
primos	madre	tío	abuelo
padre	hermana	hija	abuela

50

Family Tree

Refer to the Word Bank to write the Spanish word that matches each picture.

Word Bank
el hermano
el tío
la abuela
la hija
los primos
el hijo
la hermana
el abuelo
la madre
el padre
la familia
la tía

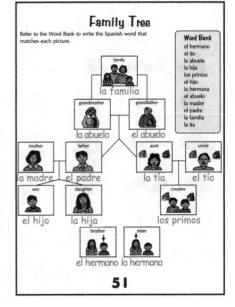

family — la familia
grandmother — la abuela   grandfather — el abuelo
mother — la madre   father — el padre   aunt — la tía   uncle — el tío
son — el hijo   daughter — la hija   cousins — los primos
brother — el hermano   sister — la hermana

51

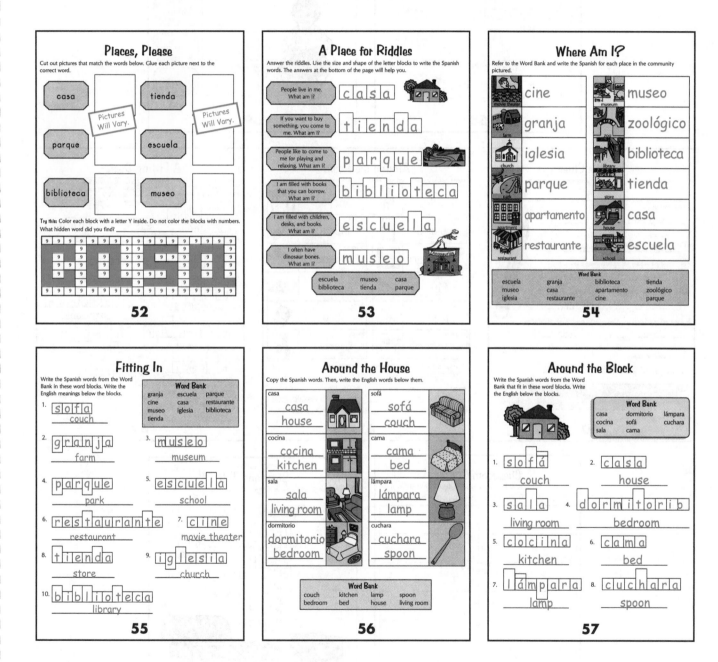

Places, Please

Cut out pictures that match the words below. Glue each picture next to the correct word.

casa	Pictures Will Vary.	tienda	Pictures Will Vary.
parque		escuela	
biblioteca		museo	

Try this: Color each block with a letter Y inside. Do not color the blocks with numbers. What hidden word did you find? _____

52

A Place for Riddles

Answer the riddles. Use the size and shape of the letter blocks to write the Spanish words. The answers at the bottom of the page will help you.

People live in me. What am I? — c a s a

If you want to buy something, you come to me. What am I? — t i e n d a

People like to come to me for playing and relaxing. What am I? — p a r q u e

I am filled with books that you can borrow. What am I? — b i b l i o t e c a

I am filled with children, desks, and books. What am I? — e s c u e l a

I often have dinosaur bones. What am I? — m u s e o

| escuela | museo | casa |
| biblioteca | tienda | parque |

53

Where Am I?

Refer to the Word Bank and write the Spanish for each place in the community pictured.

movie theater	cine	museum	museo
farm	granja		zoológico
church	iglesia	library	biblioteca
park	parque	store	tienda
apartment	apartamento	house	casa
restaurant	restaurante	school	escuela

Word Bank

escuela	granja	biblioteca	tienda
museo	casa	apartamento	zoológico
iglesia	restaurante	cine	parque

54

Fitting In

Write the Spanish words from the Word Bank in these word blocks. Write the English meanings below the blocks.

Word Bank

granja	escuela	parque
cine	casa	restaurante
museo	iglesia	biblioteca
tienda		

1. s o f a
   couch

2. g r a n j a
   farm

3. m u s e o
   museum

4. p a r q u e
   park

5. e s c u e l a
   school

6. r e s t a u r a n t e
   restaurant

7. c i n e
   movie theater

8. t i e n d a
   store

9. i g l e s i a
   church

10. b i b l i o t e c a
    library

55

Around the House

Copy the Spanish words. Then, write the English words below them.

casa — c a s a / house

sofá — s o f á / couch

cocina — c o c i n a / kitchen

cama — c a m a / bed

sala — s a l a / living room

lámpara — l á m p a r a / lamp

dormitorio — d o r m i t o r i o / bedroom

cuchara — c u c h a r a / spoon

Word Bank

| couch | kitchen | lamp | spoon |
| bedroom | bed | house | living room |

56

Around the Block

Write the Spanish words from the Word Bank that fit in these word blocks. Write the English below the blocks.

Word Bank

casa	dormitorio	lámpara
cocina	sofá	cuchara
sala	cama	

1. s o f á
   couch

2. c a s a
   house

3. s a l a
   living room

4. d o r m i t o r i o
   bedroom

5. c o c i n a
   kitchen

6. c a m a
   bed

7. l á m p a r a
   lamp

8. c u c h a r a
   spoon

57

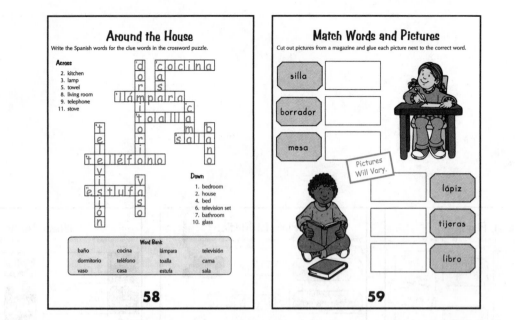

Around the House

Write the Spanish words for the clue words in the crossword puzzle.

Across
2. kitchen
3. lamp
5. towel
8. living room
9. telephone
11. stove

Crossword answers: cocina, dormitorio, casa, lámpara, toalla, escritorio, cama, baño, sala, teléfono, televisión, estufa, vaso

Down
1. bedroom
2. house
4. bed
6. television set
7. bathroom
10. glass

Word Bank			
baño	cocina	lámpara	televisión
dormitorio	teléfono	toalla	cama
vaso	casa	estufa	sala

58

Match Words and Pictures

Cut out pictures from a magazine and glue each picture next to the correct word.

silla

borrador

mesa

Pictures Will Vary.

lápiz

tijeras

libro

59

Use the Clues

Use the clues and the words at the bottom of the page. Do not use any answer more than once.

1. Both words begin with the letter *p*. You write <u>with</u> one and write <u>on</u> one. What are they?

   pluma   papel

2. You can sit at either one of these when you need to write.

   escritorio   mesa

3. You could exit through either one of these in case of fire.

   puerta   ventana

4. Both words end with the letter *o*. They both have pages.

   libro   cuaderno

5. These two words go together because one is on the end of the other.

   lápiz   borrador

6. Both words have an *i* as their second letter. One is used for cutting and the other is used for sitting.

   tijeras   silla

silla	mesa	tijeras	libro	borrador	ventana
puerta	lápiz	cuaderno	papel	escritorio	pluma

60

Around the Room

In each box, copy the Spanish word for the classroom object pictured.

silla	silla	mesa	mesa
puerta	puerta	pluma	pluma
ventana	ventana	borrador	borrador
lápiz	lápiz	cuaderno	cuaderno
papel	papel	libro	libro
escritorio	escritorio	tijeras	tijeras

Write the Spanish words from above next to the English words.

window _ventana_   chair _silla_   table _mesa_
eraser _borrador_   scissors _tijeras_   door _puerta_
desk _escritorio_   pen _pluma_   notebook _cuaderno_
paper _papel_   book _libro_   pencil _lápiz_

61

A Fitting Design

Write the Spanish words from the Word Bank that fit in these word blocks. Write the English meanings below the blocks.

Word Bank			
ventana	papel	pluma	puerta
borrador	silla	libro	cuaderno
escritorio	tijeras	mesa	lápiz

1. s i l l a — chair
2. e s c r i t o r i o — desk
3. m e s a — table
4. l á p i z — pencil
5. p a p e l — paper
6. c u a d e r n o — notebook
7. b o r r a d o r — eraser
8. l i b r o — book
9. p l u m a — pen
10. p u e r t a — door
11. v e n t a n a — window
12. t i j e r a s — scissors

62

Classroom Clutter

Draw a picture to illustrate each of the Spanish words. Refer to the Word Bank at the bottom of the page to help you.

silla	ventana
mesa	puerta
tijeras	papel
libro	cuaderno
lápiz	escritorio
borrador	pluma

Pictures Will Vary.

Word Bank				
eraser	door	scissors	pen	window	paper
chair	notebook	pencil	desk	book	table

63

Show and Tell

Write the Spanish for each clue in the crossword puzzle.

Across
1. notebook
5. scissors
7. pen
8. eraser
10. pencil
11. table
12. chair

Crossword answers: cuaderno, ventana, escritorio, tijeras, pluma, borrador, lápiz, mesa, silla

Down
2. desk
3. window
4. book
6. door
9. paper

Word Bank					
escritorio	mesa	libro	silla	tijeras	puerta
lápiz	ventana	borrador	cuaderno	papel	pluma

64

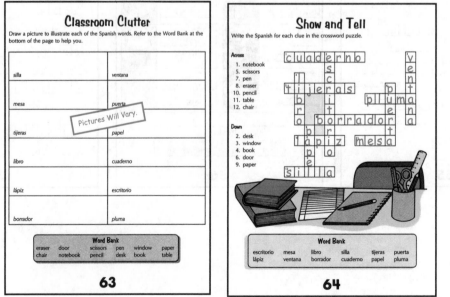

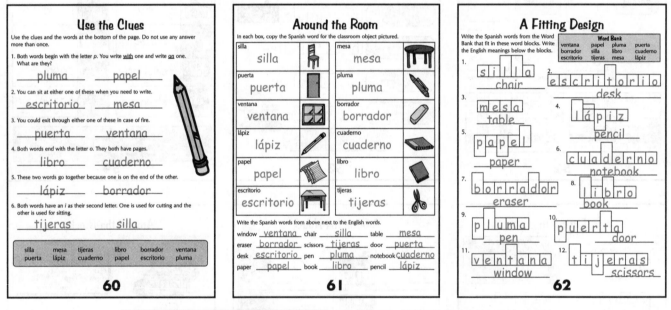